Feisty First Ladies

& OTHER UNFORGETTABLE WOMEN OF THE WHITE HOUSE

Feisty First Ladies

& OTHER UNFORGETTABLE WOMEN OF THE WHITE HOUSE

Autumn Stephens

VIVA
EDITIONS

Published in the United States by Viva Editions, an imprint of Cleis Press Inc., P.O. Box 14697, San Francisco, California 94114.

Printed in the United States.
Cover design: Scott Idleman
Text design: Frank Wiedemann
10 9 8 7 6 5 4 3 2 1

Excerpt from *Wild Women: Crusaders, Curmudgeons and Completely Corsetless Ladies in the Otherwise Virtuous Victorian Era* copyright © 1992 by Autumn Stephens. Reprinted by permission of Conari Press.

The publisher gratefully acknowledges The Library of Congress for the photos and illustrations on pages: 3, 9, 13, 17, 31, 33, 37, 43, 45, 47, 57, 61, 75, 87, 107, 109, 127, 143, 145, 157, 165, 179, 189. Photograph of Hillary Clinton on page 195: copyright: Todd Pierson, Shutterstock.com. Photograph of Laura Bush on page 201: copyright: Stocklight, Shutterstock.com. Photograph of Sarah Palin on page 207: copyright: mistydawnphoto, Shutterstock.com. Photograph of Michelle Obama on page 209: copyright: Suzanne Tucker, Shutterstock.com.

Library of Congress Cataloging-in-Publication Data

Stephens, Autumn.
Feisty first ladies and other unforgettable White House women / Autumn Stephens.
    p. cm.
ISBN 978-1-57344-356-2 (pbk. : alk. paper)
1. Presidents' spouses--United States--Biography--Anecdotes. 2. Presidents--United States--Family--Anecdotes. 3. Women--United States--Biography--Anecdotes. 4. Presidents--United States--Biography--Anecdotes. 5. White House (Washington, D.C.)--Anecdotes. 6. Washington (D.C.)--Social life and customs--Anecdotes. I. Title.

E176.2.S75 2008
973.09'9--dc22

                            2008049133

CONTENTS

* *

THOSE FORMIDABLE FEMALES

T HE CONSTITUTION IS CLEAR on the point: Technically speaking, the president of the United States, and not the woman in his life, gets to be the official Big Cheese. Yet from firebrand Abigail Adams, who exhorted the Founding Fathers to "remember the ladies" (or else!) to career woman Hillary Clinton, frankly advertised as part of the presidential package in her husband's "two-for-one" campaign, American wives, mistresses, mothers, and even serving maids over the centuries have matched the mettle of the men in the Oval Office—and, on occasion, the gall.

"The whole government is afraid of me, and well they may be," gloated early nineteenth-century reporter Anne Royall, who held a naked president's pants hostage until he granted her an interview. "Well, Warren, I have got you the presidency…what are you going to do with it?" inquired indomitable First Lady Florence Harding in 1921. And the words of audacious phone freak Martha Mitchell, who didn't hesitate in 1973 to tell Watergate conspirator Richard Nixon (and every reporter in Washington) that she had his number, still ring across the decades: "Mr. President should resign!"

Many a secret White House paramour, of course, has held (or at least briefly handled) the reins of Executive power. The careers of Presidents Thomas Jefferson, Grover Cleveland, and Dwight D. Eisenhower, to name only a few, all once hung on the question of an extramarital indiscretion (and also the forbearance of American voters).The many madcap lovers of John F. Kennedy—among them Judith Campbell Exner, also intimately involved with a Mafia boss during her two-year affair with JFK—probably deserve a book (among other things) of their own.

Not every female who infiltrates the bastion of patriarchal power, of course, revels in her role. Fiercely private Bess Truman, plagued in the mid-twentieth century by unfavorable comparisons to her larger-than-life predecessor, Eleanor Roosevelt, termed the Executive Mansion "The Great White Jail"; 150 years earlier, the much-scrutinized Martha Washington, Mother of All First Ladies, grumbled that she was "more like a state prisoner than anything else." And to the present day, savaging the president's spouse rivals football as a beloved national sport.

But for every reluctant White House resident, a dozen would-be denizens wait restlessly in the wings. Nowhere is it written, all appearances to the contrary, that the individual who inhabits the Oval Office must actually be a man: From self-proclaimed libertine Victoria Woodhull in 1872 to black feminist leader Shirley Chisholm a century later to Hilary Clinton in 2008, a host of bold trailblazers have not only fantasized about becoming president, but seriously contended for the position. And overriding the democratic process altogether, a brazen bevy of protestors, picketers, and gate-crashers—not to mention rock star Grace Slick, who once plotted to spike Richard Nixon's tea with LSD, has simply tried to take the White House by storm.

From feisty first ladies and mutinous housekeepers to overt publicity hounds and behind-the-scenes dictators, American women have left an enduring imprint in the annals of presidential history. In the spirit of 1776, here's to every White House revolutionary who celebrated Independence Day her way and to the proposition that a nation of enlightened voters will someday also "remember the ladies" at the ballot box.

I

REVOLUTIONARY FIRST
LADIES (AND A FEW SPIRITED
FRIENDS) FORGE THE WAY

MARTHA WASHINGTON

✳ ✳

A MUCH-HYPED PROTOTYPE

IF MARTHA WASHINGTON DIDN'T DO IT," observed one Clinton-era comedian of the great to-do about Hillary's hands-on approach to first ladyhood, "then no one is sure it should be done." If truth be told, however, not even Martha, the revered Mother of Her Country, escaped some rather trying eighteenth-century controversy about how to interpret her role.

Reputedly the richest woman in Virginia when she wed George in 1759, Martha, a widow of twenty-seven, reentered the state of matrimony with two small children and a slightly risqué reputation attached. Not known in her pre-George days for demureness or for dignity, she amused herself by riding her horse up and down her uncle's front steps, aggressively pursued her first husband (a wealthy tobacco farmer some twenty years her senior), and as heir to his plantation, harassed various London merchants by letter, shamelessly demanding an "uncommon Price" for her goods.

But in 1789, when Husband Number Two snagged the position of President Number One, Martha meekly turned her attention to the topic of just how the chief executive's wife should act, and also what she should be called. And so, it seems, did the rest of the just-hatched nation, then preoccupied with both the practical and the symbolic details of how to set up a democracy. The U.S. Senate convened to consider a suitable title for George, "His Highness" and "His Excellency" among the numerous options. As for his spouse, suggestions ranged from "Marquise" to "Mrs.": not until 1849 would the term "First Lady" (in reference to the deceased Dolley Madison) be verbally bandied about, and in the end, Martha remained "Lady Washington."

Regrettably, the government did not also dictate protocol to the crowds that collected in New York and Philadelphia (only with the completion of the

White House in 1800 would presidents officially reside in Washington) whenever Lady Washington stepped out her front door. "I am more like a state prisoner than anything else," the rather cranky object of curiosity complained to her sister. "...[A]s I cannot do as I like I am obstinate [and] stay home a great deal."

Even in her own drawing room, however, a critical eye was cast on Martha. To many, her approach to official entertaining (stone-faced in her seat, she nodded stiffly as female visitors curtsied at her feet) seemed a touch too Marie Antoinette. One acquaintance

Public Exhibit No. 1

derided her "awkward imitations of royalty." But the objections of a U.S. congressman took another tack. "In old countries," he carped, "a Lady of her rank would not be seen without a retinue of twenty persons."

Over two centuries after George Washington left office in 1797, Americans still hadn't managed to reach consensus concerning appropriate conduct for a presidential spouse. But from day one, the nation's premiere first partner knew exactly what to make of a perennially fickle populace. "I am still determined to be cheerful and happy in whatever situation I may be," Lady Washington wrote shortly after her husband's inauguration. But, she noted, "I have learned too much of the vanity of human affairs to expect felicity from the scenes of public life."

"There [are] certain bounds set for me which
I must not depart from..."
—MW

ABIGAIL ADAMS

✶ ✶

A FEMINIST FORERUNNER

LONG BEFORE ABIGAIL ADAMS STARTED RUNNING the country (as foes of that future first lady would one day claim), she deplored the notion that the American Revolution was supposed to be a stag affair. In 1776, when husband John joined the other Founding Fathers in Philadelphia to draw up plans for the new democracy, Abigail shot off a memorable series of firebrand missives from the couple's Massachusetts home. "Remember the ladies and be more generous and favorable to them than your ancestors!" she commanded, wickedly parodying the tone John et al took with the British. Otherwise, she warned, American women "are determined to foment a rebellion, and will not hold ourselves bound by any laws in which we have no voice or representation."

In fact, the last thing that influential Abigail (the wife of the second president and mother of the sixth) had to fear was a sudden attack of laryngitis. A prolific correspondent whose letters (some 2,000 of which survive today) bespoke her then-radical social views, she repeatedly raised her voice in support of equal educational opportunities for all—a reform resisted by men, she suggested, due to "ungenerous jealosy [sic] of rivals near the Throne." In 1774, when John was selected as a member of the Continental Congress, she insisted on being addressed as "Mrs. Delegate." "Why," she asked rhetorically, "should we not assume your titles when we give you up our names?" And in her letters, she even challenged the myth that male dominance was divinely proclaimed. "Let each planet shine in their own orbit," she wrote. "God and nature designed it so—if man is Lord, woman is Lordess—that is what I contend for."

Lordess knows, Abby tried to change her outspoken ways when Federalist leader John was elected president in 1796. But it simply wasn't in the first lady's nature "to impose a silence upon my self, when I long to talk." And thus the nation's second presidential spouse became the first (though by no means the last) to be dubbed "Mrs. President" by her enemies, while John blazed the trail for his supposedly henpecked successors as a leader who didn't "dare to make a nomination without [Abigail's] approbation."

"It is not right," sputtered a Pennsylvania senator who overheard Abigail telling John which congressmen she considered "our people," and which she most definitely did not. Naturally, the phrase "Her Majesty" came up in anti-Abigail conversations. And in 1799, after the president overrode the advice of his wife (and most of his aides as well) to send peace emissary William Murray rather than a proclamation of war to France, he himself tacitly acknowledged her influence. "O how [members of Congress] lament Mrs. A's absence," he wrote to Abigail, who had been in Boston at the time of his unpopular decision. "If she had been here, Murray would never have been named." And, he added slyly, "This ought to gratify your vanity enough to cure you."

But Abigail, who considered herself an equal partner in her husband's success, couldn't be "cured" of her feminist conceits so easily. "No man ever prospered in the world without the consent and cooperation of his wife," she observed pointedly. And while the president didn't altogether agree, he confided to his son, it was certainly better not to argue the issue. Otherwise, he whispered, Abigail was sure to "raise a rebellion."

> *"I will never consent to have our Sex considered*
> *in an inferior point of light."*
> —AA

SALLY HEMINGS

* *

DID SHE OR DIDN'T SHE?

ACCORDING TO SOME HISTORIANS, the Declaration of Independence wasn't all that Founding Father Thomas Jefferson helped conceive. For almost two hundred years, Jefferson scholars have enjoyed a steamy debate regarding allegations that the Sage of Monticello, widowed in 1782 at the age of thirty-nine, subsequently embroiled himself in a passionate love affair with Sally Hemings, the three-quarters-white slave who served as his chambermaid. In fact, the story goes, Jefferson (who professed to revile both the institution of slavery and the "amalgamation" of races) spent much of his presidency dashing back and forth between Washington and his Virginia home just so he could snuggle with Sally. "Proof" of the rumor, it was claimed, was that invariably another Hemings offspring—pale as a ghost, and often resembling Mr. Monticello himself—entered the world just about nine months after one of those amorous visits.

Whether or not there's any truth to the legend about the great statesman and so-called "sooty Sal" (a subject first publicly broached in 1802 by the suspiciously anti-Jeffersonian *Richmond Recorder),* there's no doubt that plenty of wealthy Southerners didn't think twice about sleeping with their slaves, or producing mixed-race progeny. In fact, Hemings herself (described by one of her peers as both "very handsome" and "mighty near white"), was apparently the offspring of Jefferson's father-in-law and a slave—a circumstance which made her, interestingly enough, the half-sister of Jefferson's wife.

But though no one disputes that Hemings was instrumental in running the Monticello household, the "mahogany coloured charmer" (as the *Recorder* cruelly dubbed her) was never taught to read or write, and thus recorded no clue concerning her affections—if any—for the man who was legally her master.

For nearly two hundred years, the only shred of evidence linking the purported couple was an 1873 Ohio newspaper interview with Hemings' son Madison, who suddenly saw fit, in his sixty-eighth year of life, to announce to the world that he was Thomas Jefferson's illegitimate child. Then, in 1998, DNA testing proved the existence of a genetic link between Jefferson—or a male relative of Jefferson—and at least of one of Hemings' six children.

Today, the alleged Jefferson-Hemings affair (the subject of several recent books, a PBS documentary, and the motion picture *Jefferson in Paris*) continues to stir the American imagination, with passions running strong on both sides of the controversy. The real scandal, however, is not that Jefferson may have dallied with Sally, but that more than 150 years after her death (Michelle Obama notwithstanding), the concept of a black woman so closely connected with the White House still strikes us as thoroughly exotic.

> *"Ignorance is preferable to error; and he is less remote from the truth who believes nothing, than he who believes what is wrong."*
> —Thomas Jefferson

OLD HICK'S CHICKS

Women went wild for Revolutionary War hero Andrew Jackson, the victor over John Quincy Adams in the presidential election of 1828—and a recent widower to boot. "There was something about him I cannot describe except to say that it was a presence," recalled ladyfriend Nancy Jarret, who first knew Jackson as a young law student. Her assessment was apparently shared by the throng of female admirers festooned in strands of "Old Hickory" nuts who expressed their interest (and, perhaps, their intoxication) at Jackson's inaugural by clambering feet-first onto the White House's dainty damask chairs get a good look at their 6'1", 140-pound guy.

DOLLEY MADISON

✵ ✵

A PATRIOT WITH HER OWN PRIORITIES

ALTHOUGH SHE WAS RAISED A PLAIN-LIVING QUAKER, little in Dolley Madison's jolly demeanor in 1809 suggested her austere religious background—or her famously intrepid future. Fond of naughty necklines and Turkish turbans trimmed with foot-long feathers (those astonishing headdresses alone set President James Madison back $1000 each year), the neophyte first lady cut quite a figure on the dance floor; indeed, George Washington judged her "the sprightliest partner I've ever had." Heedless of her image, she snorted snuff in public, once lecturing Senator Henry Clay on her two-handkerchief system: a large bandanna took care of the "rough work" on (or in) the nose, while a dainty lace hankie served as her "polisher."

Guests at the first lady's boisterous Wednesday evening "Squeezes," observed one legislator, included everyone from "the Minister of Russia to...the printer of a paper—greasy boots and silk stockings" notwithstanding. And among her many gal pals, the lively Lady Presidentress (as Dolley was called in her day) counted brazen Elizabeth Bonaparte, who made a big splash in deliberately dampened muslin gowns that clung to her otherwise garment-free form.

Tasty as her friends found those slightly wicked soirees, Dolley wasn't (contrary to common belief) responsible for introducing ice cream to the United States—that distinction belongs to Thomas Jefferson, who developed a taste for the frozen treat in France in the late 1700s. But, according to Charles Pinckney, two-term President Madison's vanquished rival for top office in 1808, the wildly popular first lady could certainly claim at least partial credit for her husband's political triumph. "I might have had a better chance had I faced Mr. Madison alone," Pinckney once confessed.

If it weren't for the War of 1812, however, Dolley might have gone down in history as nothing more than a fabulous Washington hostess. But when the British invaded the capital in August 1814, the doyenne of the drawing room showed her macho mettle by refusing to join the panic-stricken citizens fleeing through the streets, though both the president (who had joined his troops outside of town) and the mayor of Washington dispatched decrees commanding her to leave. "I was so unfeminine as to be free from fear," the imperturbable first lady later recalled, and she refused to abandon the White House until the sound of nearby cannon fire could no longer be ignored.

Daring Dol *en décolleté*

Even then, of course, Dolley delayed her departure long enough to pluck, in that legendary gesture of patriotism, the well-known Gilbert Stuart portrait of George Washington from the wall. We needn't worry, however, that the hitherto self-possessed Mrs. Madison, in her final moments in the Executive Mansion (torched only hours after her departure), was prepared to make the supreme sacrifice for the sake of patriarchy alone. Though the fact seldom makes it into history texts, Dolley's *final* brave act before exiting the White House was to rescue a handsome portrait of...herself.

> "There is one secret, and that is the power we all have in
> forming our own destinies."
> —DM

FROM THE INVALID TO THE INSANE

★ ★

OUT OF SIGHT FIRST LADIES

IT'S A RARE FIRST LADY WHO ACTUALLY LOOKS FORWARD to seeing her famous name splayed across the news. More often, it seems, those unelected, unpaid White House tenants must steel themselves to live gracefully (or even grudgingly) in the limelight. And even the handful of presidential spouses who, over the decades, somehow evaded the prying eye of the public nonetheless left behind a faint, poignant imprint in the nation's collective memoirs. In the most literal sense, Martha Jefferson, Rachel Jackson, Hannah Van Buren, Ellen Arthur, and Alice Lee Roosevelt never lived in the White House; none survived to see her husband assume the highest office in the land. Yet without a doubt, each of their widowers brought memories (whether sorrowful or sweet) of his departed wife with him to Washington, and beyond. Anna Harrison too, earned a brief footnote in the chronicles of this country—due to the death of her son, she was unable to attend the 1841 inauguration of husband William Henry, who himself perished barely a month thereafter.

Reclusive First Lady Letitia Tyler, who suffered a fatal stroke in the White House in 1842, shared only fleetingly in her spouse's political success. And just two months after James Garfield assumed the presidency in 1881, his wife Lucretia contracted malaria and was forced to leave Washington to convalesce; James was fatally shot in July of that year on his way to visit her at the New Jersey shore.

Invalid Ida McKinley spent the three White House years preceding her husband William's assassination in 1901 largely in seclusion, crocheting a prodigious quantity of woolen slippers. But it was not for that reason alone that her face remained unfamiliar to the nation. On the rare occasions when Ida appeared in public, she was prone to suffer an epileptic attack—an emergency that William handled by throwing a large handkerchief over her head and holding it there (meanwhile chatting nonchalantly with his guests) until the seizure passed.

Convinced that Zachary's presidency was "a plot to deprive her of his society and to shorten his life by unnecessary care and responsibility," bitter Margaret Taylor shut herself away in a second floor sitting room for sixteen months, emerging only when, just as she had predicted, her husband collapsed in office in 1850. "How I wish he was out of political life," melancholy Jane Pierce wrote shortly after her marriage to Franklin. The depression deepened when their son was killed in a train wreck just two months after Franklin's triumph in 1852, and First Lady Pierce passed the next four years secreted away in her room, writing letter after letter to her dead child.

But it was the semi-invalid Eliza Johnson, perhaps the least known first lady of all ("Her very existence is a myth to almost every one," complained one contemporary Washington writer), who spoke most eloquently on behalf of the flesh-and-blood phantoms of the White House. "It's all very well for those who like it," sighed poor Eliza, who never dreamed that her Andrew would unexpectedly succeed President Lincoln in 1865, "but I do not like this public life at all."

ELIZABETH MONROE

✭ ✭

THE HAUGHTY HERMIT

I N PARIS DURING HER HUSBAND'S TENURE as minister to France at the end of the eighteenth century, Elizabeth Monroe, "la belle Americaine," was the toast of the town. But in Washington, D.C. from 1817 to 1825, she was just plain toast, a frankly elitist first lady who had the misfortune to follow on the heels of down-to-earth, devastatingly popular Dolley Madison.

Perhaps things might have gone better for Mrs. Monroe had she, like her praiseworthy predecessor, been afforded an opportunity to snatch George Washington's portrait from the talons of advancing British soldiers. In fact, the much-maligned first lady had once rescued no mere picture, but a human political prisoner from the guillotine. Somehow, though, it was Dolley's derring-do that lingered in the mind, and not Elizabeth's intervention with French prison officials on behalf of the wife of America's Revolutionary War ally, the Marquis de Lafayette.

Elizabeth's fancy Empire furniture (later much admired by the equally patrician, but infinitely more charismatic Jacqueline Kennedy) and a taste for $1,500 French frocks certainly didn't win her many American hearts. Infinitely more galling to the public, however, was the discovery that the doctrine of hands-off-my-hemisphere wasn't promulgated by the male Monroe alone. Far from flaunting her classy possessions, Elizabeth received White House visitors with obvious reluctance, posting guards to eject anyone who didn't meet her exacting standards of dress, and turning a deaf ear to complaints that Dolley didn't do things that way.

Worse yet, she just didn't know how to properly throw a party. Contrary to the eager expectations of Washington society, only thirty guests, close family friends all, were invited to celebrate the 1820 nuptials of daughter Maria in the White House.

Nor did the recluse return the favor of the few social calls she received—one unspecified illness or another, she claimed, kept her captive in the mansion, though occasionally her older daughter was dispatched in her stead.

Today, historians speculate that Elizabeth's preference for solitude stemmed from an effort to conceal chronic epilepsy rather than from sheer unmitigated snobbery. But during the Monroe administration, snubbed

Not the neighborly type

Washington wives assumed the worst—and, in retaliation, simply scoffed at the handful of invitations they did belatedly receive from Mrs. Monroe. "The drawing room of the president," it was reported in the fall of 1819, "was opened last night to a beggarly row of empty chairs...only five females attended." And, it was further noted, three of the five "were foreigners"—who apparently didn't know any better than to humor the American first lady who mistakenly believed she was an aristocrat.

> *"In my day, if so much stir, pomp and Etiquette had been assumed the cry of Monarchy, Monarchy would have been resounded from Georgia to Maine."*
> —Abigail Adams on Elizabeth Monroe

THOSE HOSTILE D.C. HOSTESSES

✮ ✮

THE PLEASURE OF YOUR COMPANY IS REQUESTED— OR ELSE!

CAFFEINE WAS STRICTLY BESIDE THE POINT at coffee klatches in early nineteenth-century Washington. "It is understood," wrote fed-up future First Lady Louisa Adams, "that a man who is ambitious to become President of the United States must make his wife visit the Ladies of the members of Congress first. Otherwise," added the sulky socializer, who suffered through twenty-five social calls a day while her husband was in pursuit of the presidency, "he is totally inefficient to fill so high an office."

In fact, the wife of any high-ranking politician (officer seeker or no) in the early 1800s who shirked her obligations in the chat-and-chew department did so at her own peril. If there was one thing that flipped a Washington woman's wig, it was having her R.S.V.P. returned with regrets, or failing to receive a coveted call. Sooner or later, the offended lady's spouse was certain to hear all about it—and, often, to turn against the colleague whose mate had made such an egregious gaffe.

The significance of the fiercely fought female protocol wars was scarcely lost on ambitious Secretary of State John Quincy Adams. "My wife returns all visits," he worried, "but [she] adopts the principle of not visiting first any stranger who arrives, and this is what the ladies have taken in dudgeon." Nor did President James Monroe take such tiffs lightly—especially after congressmen's wives pointedly boycotted an 1819 get-together hosted by his wife Elizabeth, a solitary (and often sickly) type notorious for her failure to toe the tea party line.

More than one meeting of Monroe's Cabinet was convened to discuss "the etiquette of the visits," the upshot being a general understanding that neither Cabinet members nor their wives were actually compelled to bow to the tyranny of the tedious social call, but were "free to pursue the course of conduct dictated by their sense of propriety respectively." Human nature, however, was not profoundly altered by this noble pronouncement, and the wary invitee of Mr. Monroe's era continued, like her twentieth-century counterpart, to carefully contemplate just which side of her biscuit was apt to be buttered.

I WOULDN'T HAVE YOU
IF YOU WERE THE PRESIDENT

Later in life, Thomas Jefferson would become more proficient in the ways of wooing a woman. But in 1769, as a twenty-six-year-old bachelor, the future Founding Father tried to win the heart of one Betsey Walker by slipping torrid mash notes into her clothing while she was looking the other way. Only two small flaws spoiled the success of this unique technique: (1) its profound weirdness, and (2) the fact that his beloved was already happily married. These days, a similarly misguided suitor would probably find himself slapped with a sexual harassment suit. Times being different, however, when Jefferson persisted in this peculiar form of flirtation, Walker allegedly declared her personal independence by threatening to stab him with a pair of scissors.

LOUISA ADAMS

✫ ✫

A SPURNED SPOUSE

ACCORDING TO HER ACERBIC AUTOBIOGRAPHY, *Adventures of a Nobody,* First Lady Louisa Adams seethed with secret feminist feelings. Among the issues that incited her wrath (and sometimes her urge to write poetry as well) were sexual abuse of servant girls by their masters, slimeballs who seduced their sweethearts but failed to marry them...and the cold, insensitive tone the Adams men tended to take with their women.

Despite the sarcastic title of her tome, however, English-born Adams wasn't quite the nonentity that her spouse John Quincy seemed to assume. A fluffier first lady would never have managed, for example, to charm the charmless JQA's constituents, plan the brilliant 1824 ball that, in large part, paved the way for her husband's presidency, or soothe away stinging political criticism with the sensible advice to "put a little wool in your ears and don't read the papers." Nor, for that matter, would she have survived a terrifying sleigh journey across Russia and Poland during the winter of 1815 to meet John Quincy (then the American ambassador to Russia) in Paris. (In the end, only a cool head—and the ability to yell "Long live Napoleon" in French—saved Adams from slaughter by Napoleonic soldiers, who took her for a Russian.)

By all accounts, the tart-tongued first lady had every right to be bitter. Though she read widely, frequently attended congressional debates, and had once even considered studying astronomy, her own spouse subscribed, until late in life, to the notion that there was "something in the very nature of mental abilities which seems to be unbecoming in a female." Nearly as unbecoming as a brain, in John Quincy's antiquated book, was a bit of blush: his wife even had to fight for the right to wear rouge. No wonder that Louisa sought consolation in chocolate, nor that she brooded that "hanging and marriage were strongly assimilated." "I have nothing to do with the disposal of affairs and have never but once been consulted," she lamented.

In fact, the president may well have regretted his failure to follow the first lady's advice when she urged him to personally campaign for re-election in 1828. No amount of nagging could convince him to lift a finger on his own behalf, and JQA was defeated, of course, by the dashing Andrew Jackson. In the view of Mrs. Adams, however, the loss was less than devastating. After a lifetime in the public eye, the perpetually frustrated first lady was ready to hang up her hat in private.

Chocolate lover Louisa Adams

Besides, if nothing else, her husband's defeat afforded Adams the undisputed right to invoke the most satisfying marital mantra known to humankind: "See, dear, didn't I tell you so?"

> *"I was carried through my journey and trials by the mercy of a kind Providence, and by the conviction that weakness, either of body or mind, would only render my difficulties greater and make matters worse."*
> —LA

MARY CATHERINE HELLEN

✶ ✶

THE KISSING COUSIN

THOUGH THERE WERE A FEW MEMBERS OF THE CLAN who didn't care for her, Mary Catherine Hellen never met an Adams she didn't like. The boy-crazy cousin to the three sons of President John Quincy and First Lady Louisa Adams, devil-may-care Mary Catherine bewitched the youngest, bamboozled the eldest, and seems to have been, for a time, betrothed to two of the brothers at once.

The Curse of Mary Catherine was first visited upon the Adams household in 1820, when the thirteen-year-old coquette-in-training set her cap for the youngest son, Charles Francis, whose greatest appeal at the time may have consisted of his geographical proximity. But when big brother George (a promising Harvard law student, and a sensitive poet into the bargain) came home to Washington, Mary Catherine no longer found Charles Francis quite so fascinating. In fact, by the summer of 1823, she and George were engaged, and a chastened Charles Francis confided to his diary that he could "never expect similar happiness again."

But George's euphoria, too, was to be fleeting—his fatal mistake was assuming that his fickle fiancée would wait patiently in Washington while he returned to Boston for "perhaps five or six years" until he got on his feet financially. Like a fly in heat, Mary Catherine was soon buzzing around Charles Francis again, and the once-sorrowful sibling gloated in his journal that "George...would be in a perfect fever and sickness if he was to imagine that she had encouraged me in the least."

In 1825, John Quincy Adams assumed the office of president, and he and his brood (including beloved cousin Mary Catherine) moved into the White House, where it apparently came to the attention of George's fiancée and Charles

Francis' heart-throb that she hadn't yet sampled the wares of the middle son, John. Though her latest Adams acquisition had recently been expelled from Harvard and was deeply drawn to the bottle, Mary Catherine soon found that she couldn't get enough of him. "Of one thing I am satisfied, that Mary has been behaving unworthily to George," glowered Charles Francis, left—like George—in the cold once again.

Following a prolonged and often precarious betrothal, Mary Catherine and John Adams were married in February of 1828 at an elegant evening ceremony in the White House. Neither George (who, suffering from symptoms of "mental alienation," would soon either leap or fall to his death) nor the oft-victimized Charles Francis was present to wish the couple well. And even First Lady Louisa Adams, Mary Catherine's aunt/new mother-in-law, could summon little enthusiasm for the event. "John looks already as if he had all the cares in the world upon his shoulders..." she wrote shortly after the wedding. Not so, however, the world's undisputed authority on the Adams men, her hooks now forever embedded in the famous family flesh. "Madame," noted the nerve-wracked mother of Charles Francis, John, and George, "is cool easy and indifferent as ever."

> *"...One of the most capricious women that were ever formed in a capricious race...!"*
> —Charles Francis Adams on his much-loved cousin Mary Catherine

ANNE ROYALL

✮ ✮

A PAIN IN THE PRESIDENTIAL PANTS

NINETEENTH-CENTURY NEWSWOMAN ANNE ROYALL failed to faint when she came across the utterly unclad President John Quincy Adams taking his daily dip in the Potomac one morning, his clothes piled in a vulnerable little heap on the shore. Instead, so the story goes, Royall— the gray-haired widow of a wealthy Revolutionary War veteran—plopped her posterior down on the presidential pants and refused to budge until he granted her a long-coveted interview.

Whether or not that bizarre in-the-buff press conference actually occurred (some historians pooh-pooh the idea that Royall, a long-term pal of the president, needed to play dirty pool to land her story), it's clear that the late-blooming journalist—a seasoned soul of fifty-four before she published a word—exerted a formidable force on friends and enemies alike.

"While other lady writers dipped their quills in treacle, Anne Royall more often dipped hers in bile," wrote one biographer of the geriatric gazetteer who was acquainted, remarkably, with all fourteen presidents from Washington to Pierce. But her tongue could be treacherous too—Royall so annoyed one stranger with her unsolicited remarks that he threw her down the stairs, shattering her leg in the process. She harangued big-top buddy P.T. Barnum on his misguided political preferences until he fled in fear, going out of his way to ensure that he "never again met the eccentric old lady." And on one historical occasion in 1829, Royall was driven to denounce evangelist clergyman John Coyle as "a damned old bald-headed son of a bitch," after he prayed aloud for her conversion. As it turned out, her assessment of Coyle's character, if not the state of his pate, wasn't far off the mark: rather than turning the other cheek, the miffed minister hauled Royall into the Court of the District of Columbia, where she was tried and convicted of the crime of being "a common scold."

Apparently more inspired than deterred by her sex-specific rap sheet, sixty-two-year-old Royall went on to found (and, often, strong-arm subscribers to) the acerbic widely read Washington weekly *Paul Pry,* in whose pages few politicians were spared her stinging barbs. (Vice President Martin Van Buren, she once opined, "is obnoxious to all parties because there is no dependence to be placed on the man...like the Irishman's flea, when you put your hand on him he is not there.")

But Royall's most inspired invective was reserved for her personal enemies in the evangelical movement—the hypocritical "Hallelujah Holdforths" she accused of corrupting Native American culture, plotting to take over the government, and various other doings so dark as to be almost completely obscure. "Let all pious booksellers who take pious bribes beware," she wrote in 1832. "Let all pious young ladies who hawk pious tracts into young gentlemen's rooms beware." And, warned the sexagenarian terror of the Potomac, "let all pious Generals, Colonels and Commanders of our army and navy who make war upon old women beware."

"The whole government is afraid of me, and well they may be."

—AR

RACHEL JACKSON

✮ ✮

THE BIGAMIST BRIDE

T HOUGH RACHEL JACKSON WAS A SOBER CITIZEN of sixty-two in 1828, devoted only to her church and her man, many Americans were persuaded that the wife of war hero Andrew Jackson was, for reasons of moral turpitude, utterly unfit to inhabit the presidential mansion.

In fact, risqué Rachel's only real vice seems to have been her fondness for puffing on a clay pipe in the privacy of her own home—an unattractive habit, perhaps, but scarcely a degenerate one. Indeed, loyal Andrew once even fought a lethal (for the other party) pistol duel in defense of her honor. But thanks to a smear campaign designed to discourage her husband's designs on the office held by President John Quincy Adams, Rachel's reputation as an adulteress, a bigamist, and (as one particularly ringing epithet had it) "an American Jezebel," grew more shocking by the day.

Like most rumors, the scuttlebutt about the wanton ways of the "profligate" wife sprang from a tiny kernel of truth: technically speaking, Rachel had indeed been, for a brief time, simultaneously wed to two men. But the circumstances couldn't have been more mitigating—she and Andrew married in 1791 under the mistaken impression that her divorce from an abusive first husband was a done deed. In fact, the proceedings weren't finalized for another two years, and when the situation came to light in 1794, the Jacksons simply tied the knot again—this time without a hitch.

The rather innocuous facts notwithstanding, however, Rachel remained one of the most reviled public figures of her day, the subject of vicious attacks not only on her character, but also her lack of beauty or grace. According to one snide report, her stout figure "show[ed] how far the skin can be stretched"; a glimpse of Rachel dancing at a ball evoked the comparison to a "short, fat dumpling bobbing" up and down. Painfully aware that her appearance was not an asset to her husband's career Rachel belatedly called in an advisor to perform a sartorial update and tutor her in social skills.

Andrew's victory in November 1828, however, was bittersweet at best, as the newly (if not entirely successfully) made-over matron had already paid a stiff price for her husband's presidency, and dreaded the savage scrutiny that four years in the White House were certain to bring. "I had rather be a doorkeeper in the house of God than live in that palace at Washington," she lamented to friends. For better or worse, Rachel got her wish: she died of a heart attack in December 1828, just weeks before her husband was to take office, and was buried in the white gown she had purchased for his inauguration—a garment, it was noted with characteristic cruelty, "more suitable for a young and beautiful bride."

> *"The enemys of the Genls have dipt their arrows in*
> *wormwood & gall and sped them at me."*
> —RJ

PEGGY EATON

✷✷✷✷✷✷✷✷✷✷✷✷✷✷✷✷✷✷✷✷✷✷✷✷✷✷✷✷

THE CURSE OF ANDREW JACKSON'S CABINET

D OLLEY MADISON, FOR ONE, didn't find twelve-year-old Peggy Eaton (née O'Neale) a menace to society when she crowned her the dancing school queen of D.C. in 1811. Three years later, when Peggy waltzed right on out the door to elope (ultimately unsuccessfully, it turned out) with an army officer, all it meant was that she was light on her feet. And even her marriage at seventeen to John Timberlake, a good-looking gentleman with whom she'd been acquainted precisely two weeks, wasn't enough to set tongues wagging. Whatever else could be said about Peg's eagerness to wed, at least she'd never suffer from the socially unattractive condition of nineteenth-century spinsterhood.

But two years later, when single Senator John Eaton of Tennessee took up residence in her papa's boardinghouse (where Peggy helped out as a hostess), gossips finally had enough grist for their mill. Washington was aghast when the senator convinced Timberlake to take a berth on a four-year sea voyage in 1824, then started squiring his Mrs. hither and yon. And when the poor sailor contracted T.B. on the journey and died, the public outcry was shrill enough to pierce the White House walls.

With rumors ricocheting all over town that Peggy's cuckolded spouse had actually been driven to suicide, President Andrew Jackson could see that his plan to appoint his old friend Senator Eaton to a Cabinet post wasn't destined to please. But the president, who blamed scandal-mongering for the early demise of his own wife Rachel (widely slandered as a bigamist), refused to hear a word against the senator and his lady friend. "Marry Peg forthwith," he commanded Eaton in 1828, and proceeded to name him secretary of war.

Connubial bliss for Peggy and her second mate, however, was destined to be of the most abbreviated sort. Sanctimonious socialites cut her at every turn, and President Jackson's own niece, then acting as his official hostess, refused to acknowledge her at all. Infuriated by the snub, Jackson sent his relative packing and boldly seated Mrs. Eaton next to him at the next White House dinner, thereby inspiring the inventive rumor that promiscuous Peggy was now also the president's lover.

But the brouhaha over one woman's marital history wasn't confined solely to the social realm. Indeed, so severely did the controversy split Jackson's Cabinet (the secretary of state, for one, threatened to resign over the issue) that Eaton voluntarily vacated his appointment in 1831 to spare the president further anguish. By that time, however, Jackson had reached the end of his endurance and summarily demanded the resignations of all advisors who questioned Mrs. Eaton's morals.

Not the least chastened by her wretched reputation, irrepressible Peggy continued to scandalize Washington society to the end of her days—even managing, as a widow of sixty, to elope with her granddaughter's nineteen-year-old dancing teacher. And as usual, the busybodies who loudly deplored the latest development in the deliciously shocking saga had it all wrong: if every woman in the public eye modeled herself after Mother Teresa, what would less interesting individuals ever have to talk about?

"Age cannot wither her, nor custom stale her infinite virginity."
—Daniel Webster (paraphrasing Shakespeare)
on the ever-fascinating subject of Peggy Eaton's virtue

THE HAUNTED HOUSE

✰ ✰

WASHINGTON'S MOST TENACIOUS TENANTS

EVEN IN DEATH, AN UNEASY ABRAHAM LINCOLN continues to cast his 6' 4" shadow over the White House—or so, over the years, numerous residents and guests have claimed. Among the many cool customers who have allegedly seen or sensed the lanky apparition: Grace Coolidge, Eleanor Roosevelt, and Queen Wilhelmina of the Netherlands. But though Lincoln may be the least publicity-shy spirit to roam the White House halls, distinguished D.C. ectoplasm isn't limited exclusively to the male form.

For Abigail Adams, who used to hang her laundry in the unfinished East Room to dry, a woman's work is evidently never done: though Abby passed on in 1818, she reportedly still shows up every now and then to check on the state of her wash. Frances Cleveland, who in 1893 became the first president's wife to give birth in the White House, apparently also labors eternally: from time to time, she disturbs the sleep of the living with her anguished groans. And bossy Florence Harding, who, according to her henpecked husband, made his life a living "Hell" until his death in 1923, still traumatizes the timid with her dramatic wails and moans.

Setting impossible standards even in the afterworld, busy Dolley Madison, who departed this life in 1849, doesn't limit her spectral appearances solely to the White House, although she allegedly raised quite an on-site ruckus when Edith Wilson dug up her old flower garden in the early twentieth century. Dolley's second happy haunting ground, according to some, is a nearby Washington home, built in the shape of an octagon and purportedly once connected to the White House by an underground passageway. As the story goes, when the first lady fled the presidential manor as the British advanced in 1814, it was through this secret corridor that she ran, and the supernatural thumps and bumps that still echo throughout the octagonal residence result from Dolley's failure (nineteen decades of practice notwithstanding) to keep a firm grip on George Washington's portrait as she scampers toward safety.

In the White House as elsewhere, however, many spooks prove to be of the self-exorcising sort. With much malice aforethought, Woodrow Wilson's three ghastly girls enjoyed lurking in dark corners in order to startle unsuspecting visitors. The rather petite phantom that plagued the administration of William Taft turned out to be the very material daughter of a White House maid—or so Lillian Parks, who once wore a white dress as she accompanied her mother on her evening rounds, confessed in her 1961 memoirs. And with all due respect to the restless dead, even the most zombie-phobic visitor to 1600 Pennsylvania Avenue probably has more to fear, historically speaking, from its official occupants than any phantasmagoric first lady still peeved about some nineteenth-century turn of events. As Alice Roosevelt Longworth (who frequented the Executive Mansion during the reign of the Taft-era wraith and lived to tell the tale) once noted: "There are worse things than ghosts. Bad presidents in the White House are worse than apparitions."

II

QUEEN VICTORIA'S QUIRKY AMERICAN CONTEMPORARIES

JULIA TYLER

✶ ✶

THE LAST LAUGH

MOST MARRIAGE-MINDED YOUNG WOMEN in the 1840s would have considered the president of the United States a reasonably decent catch. But twenty-three-year-old Julia Gardiner, the daughter of a New York senator, wasn't so sure that her suitor John Tyler was the man she wanted to wed. For one thing, Ms. Gardiner (who positively dazzled Washington during the 1843 social season) also had proposals from two congressmen and Supreme Court Justice John McLean to ponder. In addition, a German nobleman had offered his hand, as had numerous English beaux who, noted one contemporary writer, "upon meeting her seemed suddenly to become aware of the value of their lost colonies." And finally, the apple of John's fifty-three-year-old eye also counted the president's age-appropriate son as one of her admirers.

Under the amenable circumstances, the much-romanced "Rose of Long Island" (as she styled herself) saw no need to settle on any one prospect with haste. But John, a widower of five months' duration when he set his heart on Julia in 1843, proved so eager to forge an alliance that he chased her around a White House table in pursuit of an initial kiss. ("It was truly amusing," observed Julia's sister Margaret, who happened to witness the scene.) The fun and games continued at George Washington's Birthday Ball that year, when Julia graciously declined John's proposal by giggling "No, no, no," and tossing her head so that the streamer hanging from her hat repeatedly smacked him in the head. "It amused me to see the expression on his face as he tried to make love to me and the tassle brushed his face," she later smirked. And the entire Gardiner family got a few laughs out of the president's love letters (rife with poetic references to "raven tresses" and "brightest roses"), which Julia enjoyed reading aloud.

In February of 1844, however, the accidental death of Julia's father during a pleasure cruise on the Potomac—an event witnessed by both Julia and John—served to deepen her feelings. Stunned by the spectacle, Julia fainted into John's arms—and afterward, she later told reporter Nellie Bly, "I felt differently toward the president." The two were secretly married in New York in June of that year, and soon it was the turn of the press, which had been informed only that John was taking a rest from his "arduous duties," to be amused. "We rather think the President's 'arduous duties' are only begin-

The jolly June bride

ning," snickered a reporter for the *New York Herald* (who could not, however, have possibly foreseen that the unlikely May-December union would eventually produce seven children).

As for Julia, she took to her new position like a queen to the throne, greeting official guests with a faux crown on her head and a dozen handmaids by her side, dancing with abandon (and also with any gentleman who asked) at gala White House parties, and crowing that "last night at least fifty members of Congress paid their respects to me" after one particularly successful fete. "I have commenced my auspicious reign," gloated the bride who played hard to get, "and am in quiet possession of the Presidential mansion."

"[John Tyler] seemed...to be more agreeable in every way than any young man ever was or ever could be."
—JT

SARAH POLK

★ ★

A HANDS-ON HELPMATE

WHEN JAMES POLK POPPED THE QUESTION in the early 1820s, his teenage sweetheart Sarah didn't exactly swoon at his feet. The future first lady did make it clear, however, that the Democrat's proposal would meet with more favor if he first made a name for himself in the Tennessee legislature. And from that day on (yes, in 1823 the president-to-be won both a seat in the House of Representatives and his pragmatic girlfriend's hand), Sarah Polk never stopped calling the shots for Jim.

A person of steel-plated Calvinist principles, "Sahara Sarah" did not make partying a major priority—and therefore, she let it be known, neither would James. Due to her influence, there was no great revelry for President Polk on his inaugural day in 1845; the band fell silent, and the mood turned chill, when the new first lady showed up at the celebratory fete. At Sarah's direction, no wine was ever poured for White House guests. As for evening entertainment: "How indecorous it would seem for dancing to be going on in one apartment," she gasped, "while in another we were conversing with dignitaries of the republic or ministers of the gospel." And woe unto the visitor who dared show up on the Sabbath. One Austrian diplomat was summarily turned away, while other less fortunate guests were pressed into attending church services with the first couple.

In matters political, however, austere Sarah waxed positively passionate. "If I get to the White House, I will neither keep house nor make butter," she vowed during the campaign of 1844, and James' wife was a woman of her word. Leaving tedious domestic details to others (admittedly an easier feat for childless Sarah than for many of her peers), she labored side by side with the president, previewing his reading material for items of importance, composing his correspondence, and even influencing, according to one historian, his expansionist "Manifest Destiny" policy.

When Cabinet members came to call, it was noted, the first lady "was always present." Female visitors, complained one Washington wife, were left to cool their heels in the sitting room, while the hostess "was always in the parlor with Mr. Polk" and other male guests. And the president, who never assembled a kitchen cabinet, or relied on the advice of a trusted aide, made no effort to conceal how significant he found the assistance of his spouse. "None but Sarah knew so intimately my private affairs," he conceded.

The Hell with housework

Regrettably, First Lady Sarah never made it to the famous women's rights convocation at Seneca Falls in 1848. According to one presidential scholar, she most likely encouraged her husband to attend. But as the spouse of the most overtly influential first lady ever to occupy the White House to that date, James Polk scarcely needed to brush up on the basic tenets of feminism. Nor, one suspects, would he have disagreed in the slightest with the contemporary politician who observed that strong-willed Sarah was "certainly mistress of herself"—and, he noted coyly, "I suspect of somebody else also."

"I always take a deep interest in State and national affairs."
—SP

HARRIET LANE

✶ ✶

THE HELPFUL HETEROSEXUAL

W HOEVER HEARD IN ALL HIS LIFE OF a candidate without a wife?" So ran the nasty doggerel dreamed up by opponents of life-long bachelor James B. Buchanan, the sixty-five-year-old Democratic presidential nominee in the campaign of 1856. Despite his spouseless state, however, Buchanan managed to beat out John C. Fremont and Millard Fillmore for the dubious pleasure of occupying the White House while the country teetered on the verge of civil war. And, thanks to Harriet Lane, the dazzling twenty-seven-year-old niece with the deep décolletage who served as the president's surrogate wife in every particular but one, the Buchanan administration didn't suffer from want of a feminine touch.

In fact, matrimony-shy Uncle James might well (as some contemporaries suggested) have preferred a masculine person as his partner. One commentator was especially blunt: with his "shrill, female voice, and wholly beardless cheeks," it observed, Buchanan was not "the sort of man likely to cut, or attempt to cut throat for a Chloe or Phillis [sic]…" And it did not go unnoted when "Betsy Buchanan" (as one vicious critic termed the chief of state) became excessively possessive vis-à-vis the attentions of a married member of his Cabinet.

Even effeminate Uncle James, however, couldn't compete with Harriet—who, in 1853, had made a big splash in the court of Queen Victoria—in the glamour-girl department. Known for her white satin gowns and seriously plunging neck-lines (the latter soon much in vogue), Ms. Lane treated herself to huge bouquets of roses, drained every last cent (and maybe then some) of a congressional appropriation to decorate the White House in high Victorian style, and lobbied to have her portrait included in a European register of nobility.

Not only did Harriet (the first White House hostess ever referred to in print as the "first lady") serve her uncle by bringing "the highest degree of elegance" to state social events, however, but her own romantic exploits provided plenty of distracting heterosexual dish for gossipmongers. Edward, the roguish Prince of Wales, was treated to a personal Washington tour by the president's niece—and also soundly trounced at bowling. Another swain who ventured that her handsome hands were "fitted to play the harp" was startled by Harriet's suggestive response that they might also "awaken to ecstasies the living lyre." And no doubt Washington made much of the fact that the sophisticate who had once spurned a European noble was in no particular hurry to settle down (though not, evidently, for the same reasons as her uncle), and found her frequent marriage proposals "dreadfully troublesome."

Although perhaps the oddest couple ever to preside over the White House (and, in their own way, pioneers in the concept of family values), James and Harriet certainly never achieved the same prominent position in the Presidential Hall of Fame as their successors, the Lincolns. Still, the fussy old bachelor and his devoted, bosom-baring niece managed to carve out a memorable niche for themselves. Buchanan's four years in office (the last frivolous hurrah before the nation plunged into war) would one day be remembered by old-timers as, appropriately enough, "that gayest administration."

"Uncle...places such confidence in me that he gives himself no uneasiness."
—HL

MARY LINCOLN

* *

THE WINNER OF OUR DISCONTENT

TODAY, MANIACAL MARY LINCOLN WOULD BE the self-dramatizing star of some Beltway twelve-step program, or popping Prozac like miniature petit fours, or holding an Oprah audience in thrall with tales of how an ungrateful nation did her wrong. Or maybe the stressed-out, spendthrift first lady who landed herself in hot water for running over the White House redecorating budget would simply max out her plastic while tuned to the Home Shopping Channel.

But back in March of 1861, when temperamental Mother Lincoln stormed into Washington on the stringy arm of Honest Abe, self-indulgent behavior ran distinctly counter to the restrained Victorian vein. To "Mrs. President Lincoln," as Mary rather grandly called herself (others could think of different terms), however, immediate gratification was a way of life.

"Mrs. Lincoln wanted what she wanted when she wanted it and no substitute!" sniffed White House insider Julia Taft, and stories that confirmed her remark were rampant. On her way to Washington for her husband's inauguration, Mary stopped in New York to order sixteen fancy frocks in a misguided attempt to impress a nation on the brink of war, and would tolerate no commentary on her unfortunate extravagance. "I want the women to mind their own business," she snapped. "I intend to wear what I please." Spying a handsome bit of ribbon trimming the hat of an acquaintance, she commanded the startled woman to strip the decor from her chapeau so she could affix it to her own. On occasions when a new ensemble was delivered late, or perhaps in imperfect condition, the first lady (then in her mid-forties), would fling herself kicking and screaming to the floor. And after the sudden death of her eleven-year-old son in 1862, Mary's ravings became so severe that many branded her a lunatic.

Nearly as fond of dressings down as dressing up, the first lady often fired her domestic help on whim. After booting the steward, she suggested that she receive his salary in her capacity as chief caretaker of the White House. And indeed, she could have put that sum to good use: though the president went to his grave without suspecting a thing, Mary's garment-gathering sprees eventually landed her nearly $30,000 in debt. Nonetheless, while other war-conscious women (so one newswriter noted) "sewed, scraped lint," and "made bandages," Mary "spent her time rolling to and fro between Washington and New York, intent on extravagant purchases for herself..." The rumor even circulated that staff was being sacrificed for the great and glorious cause of Mary Lincoln's wardrobe, and, eventually, the first lady's mail was so overrun with poison-pen letters that she had to ask a clerk to screen it for her.

A conspicuous consumer

"I do not belong to the public; my character is wholly domestic, and the public have nothing to do with it," Mary protested as her ill-repute soared to unprecedented heights. As usual, however, the chronically out-of-touch first lady was dead wrong. Like each and every one of her peers, even pathologically self-centered Mary Lincoln couldn't call her soul her own while her husband served in office—a fact that all the Prozac in America would have been powerless to alter.

"Oh, it is no use to make any defense; all such efforts would only make me a target for new attacks."
—ML

WHAT KIND OF MONSTER
WAS MARY LINCOLN?

"[T]he tales that are told of Mrs. Lincoln's vanity, pride, vulgarity and meanness ought to put any decent man or woman to the blush."

—The *Sacramento Union*

"[A] coarse, vain, unamiable woman [with] the peevish assurance of a baseless parvenue"

—The *Illinois Register*

"They say Mrs. L is awfully western, loud & unrefined."

—Harriet Lane, *White House hostess*

"The weak minded Mrs. Lincoln had her bosom on exhibition, and a flower pot on her head, while there was a train of silk dragging on the floor behind her…"

—Oregon senator

"There is no denying the fact that she is a curiosity…She is not easy to get along with…"

—Commissioner B.B. French

"[D]eranged for years, and should be pitied for all her strange acts."

—The *Springfield Journal*

"[N]o more insane than I am."

—Myra Bradwell, the first woman admitted to the Illinois bar

RUTHLESS CAPITALISM

Someday, perhaps, patriotic (or just plain weird) snackers will be able to enjoy a Chelsea Chew, or munch a handful of Almond Amy Crunch. But don't start salivating just yet. Back in 1920, Chicago confectioner Otto Schnering came up with a new, improved version of his standard fudge roll and remarketed it as the "Baby Ruth." Then as now, everyone assumed that the appellation was a blatant attempt to capitalize on the famous name of twenty-five-year-old baseball great Babe Ruth. Schnering's lawyers, however, swore up and down that the confection was meant to commemorate the long-deceased daughter of former president Grover Cleveland, and the "Baby Ruth" candy bar still grips the foods-named-after-first-daughters market in a savage stranglehold today.

THOSE WIMPY WASHINGTON WIVES

When Oliver Wendell Holmes was appointed to the Supreme Court in 1902, Theodore Roosevelt welcomed him to Washington with a big White House bash. But Justice Holmes' straight-shooting spouse, Fanny, didn't quite rise to the spirit of the occasion. When Teddy tried to make polite (if somewhat sexist) small talk, inquiring how she liked the charming local ladies, Fanny committed the faux pas of failing to take the Fifth. "Washington," she indiscreetly informed her well-meaning host, "is full of famous men and the women they married when they were young."

BEYOND THE POLITICAL PALE

★ ★

THAT ALL-AMERICAN SPIRIT

SEANCES IN THE SOLARIUM, PSYCHICS ON THE PHONE, astrologers practically pitching their tents on the White House lawn...What's the world coming to? That, of course, is the million dollar question that's sent many a freaked-out first lady (among them Julia Tyler, Julia Grant, Edith Wilson, and allegedly Betty Ford) in frantic search of the sort of advice that your average political consultant just can't provide...

MARY LINCOLN DIDN'T MAKE A MOVE without consulting her medium—and, if she'd had her way, neither would her man. Alerted by clairvoyant Madame Laurie to the alarming fact that "the Cabinet were all enemies of the president, working for themselves," Mary begged Abe in vain to lose those loutish advisors. On the subject of his safety, however, the fearful first lady might have managed to get her husband's ear—both Lincolns had premonitions of his violent death. Not so, apparently, Madame Laurie, who failed to predict that April 14, 1865 might not be the best evening for Mr. and Mrs. Lincoln to attend the theater. Mary's alternative belief system also proved to be a big minus for the judge who had the former first lady institutionalized in 1875 on the grounds of insanity.

★ ★ ★

IN THE EARLY 1920s, DABBLING IN THE OCCULT was very much in vogue—even First Lady Florence Harding (plus several U.S. senators' wives) swore by a Washington astrologer known as Madame Marcia. Probably Mme. M., who discreetly entered and exited the White House via the back door, didn't need a crystal ball to see that Flo's ever-philandering Warren would have "many clandestine love affairs." Equally accurate, though far more uncanny, was the celebrated stargazer's prediction that Warren wouldn't live to finish his term—a forecast that haunted Florence, but did nothing to help her change the future.

⋆ ⋆ ⋆

THE PRECAUTIONARY PREDICTIONS of Nancy Reagan's astrologer, Joan Quigley, allegedly saved Ronnie from the grievous fate of presidents Lincoln and Harding. Thanks to her planetary savvy, Quigley bragged, Ronald Reagan was "the only president elected in a zero-numbered year that didn't die in office" since 1841. Quigley also drew praise (albeit faint) from presidential aide Michael Deaver, a man intimately acquainted with Nancy's history of seeking paranormal advice. "At least this astrologer is not as kooky as the last one," Deaver conceded.

⋆ ⋆ ⋆

IN 1996, FIRST LADY HILLARY CLINTON, previously pilloried for her lack of interest in baking cookies, suffered another P.R. setback when word got out that on occasion she wondered what her heroine Eleanor Roosevelt (deceased since 1962) would do in her shoes. By all accounts, Hill's rap sessions with the Big El were purely hypothetical—absolutely no spirit conjuring or Ouija boards involved. Along the same lines, Jacqueline Kennedy used to commune with Honest Abe in the Lincoln Room. "I'd sort of be talking with him," Jackie once claimed, "I could really feel his strength." Historic precedent notwithstanding, the press had a field day with the fact that Hillary's pal Jean Houston, who originally suggested the stress-reducing exercise, was known as a "psychic" philosopher. Needless to say, if Houston's extrasensory powers (or, for that matter, those of any of her White House predecessors) were truly up to par, she would have warned the first lady off the whole business in the first place.

JULIA GRANT

✳ ✳

NO GENERAL COMPLAINTS

HAD FIRST LADY-TO-BE JULIA GRANT heeded her parents, she never would have married Ulysses S. in 1848. According to Julia's dad, a Missouri plantation owner, his precious first-born daughter (her crossed eyes and plain looks notwithstanding) could certainly land a better catch than the ne'er-do-well twenty-six-year-old West Point graduate. And just as Pop predicted, Ulysses proved an abysmal provider, failing first as a farmer, then as an entrepreneur, and, most humiliating of all, finally winding up as a clerk in his own father's harness shop.

But in the end, of course, Julia's choice paid off: during the Civil War, her husband found his forte on the battlefield, and in 1868, the United States rewarded the victorious Union general by making him its eighteenth president. "Now, my dear," the nation's Republican leader whispered to his spouse, seconds after he was sworn in, "I hope you're satisfied." And indeed, Mrs. Grant (in contrast to so many first ladies before and since) found absolutely no fault with her prestigious new domain. "It was quite the happiest period of my life," she later recalled of her years as mistress of the presidential mansion.

Despite a self-professed lack of political acumen (a trait that historians today claim she shared with the president), Julia promptly proceeded to instruct her husband on how to fill his Cabinet. Secretary of State Hamilton Fish received his post largely because she liked his wife, while gentlemen who did not find favor were quickly bounced from positions of power. According to some calculations, in fact, no other first lady would ever influence so many dismissals, and Ulysses joked that he had to hide his list of intended appointments to keep it intact.

In the social realm, however, Julia proved the most egalitarian of hostesses, much to the delight of Washingtonians who never caught so much as a glimpse of her predecessor, the reclusive Eliza Johnson. No one save for ladies so sloppy as to show up without hats was banned from Julia's jam-packed receptions, held not once, but twice a week. "Chambermaids elbowed countesses," reported one partygoer, "and all enjoyed themselves." In contrast to Mary Lincoln, savaged for the slightest extravagance during the Civil War eight years before, Julia drew only praise for her staggering twenty-nine course dinners, enlivened by a potent trademark punch of champagne and Cointreau. And though Mrs. Grant had the dubious distinction, more than a century

One happy hostess

before First Lady Hillary Clinton, of enduring an inconclusive Congressional investigation into her financial affairs, her popularity never flagged.

Unfortunately for Julia, the same electorate that found her gregarious charm so compelling was less impressed with the administration of her spouse, and in 1876, after two increasingly scandal-ridden terms in office, the Hero of Appomattox was pointedly not renominated by his party. "I feel like a waif," the first lady wailed as she left Washington. And though the Grants were treated, on their grand tour of the globe later that year, as the equals of every monarch that they met, no subsequent experience could ever compare to Julia's eight-year tenure as first lady. "I wish it might have continued forever," she sighed wistfully, "except that it would have deterred others from enjoying the same privilege."

"I had enjoyed my independence too long to submit quietly."
—JG

VICTORIA WOODHULL

✶ ✶

ANOTHER PROMISCUOUS WOULD-BE PRESIDENT

IN THE OPINION OF VICTORIA WOODHULL, the nation's first female presidential candidate, it was no coincidence that she and the famous British queen across the Atlantic shared a common moniker. "I believe...in the fatality of triumph as somehow inherited in my name," she declared in 1872, and took to dressing in royal purple in preparation for her anticipated White House reign.

Suffice it to say that Queen Victoria would not have been amused. Their mutual appellation, it turned out, wasn't all that the chosen candidate of the Equal Rights Party in 1872 believed in: pleasure without procreation, sex without spouses, and prostitution without imprisonment all received her enthusiastic endorsement. "I am a free lover!" Woodhull liked to boast. And clearly she practiced what she preached, simultaneously sharing her New York home with a derelict ex-husband and a subsequent, more satisfactory beau—and that wasn't nearly the entire list of Mrs. W's many loves.

Then too, the sexy candidate's checkered resume, which included a stint as the fortune-telling Madame Harvey and allegedly another as a harlot, was enough to make even the boldest monarch blush. Even if Woodhull didn't actually try her hand at the oldest profession in the world, she certainly experimented with one of the most novel: in 1870, she and sister Tennessee Claflin founded a Wall Street brokerage firm with aging millionaire Cornelius Vanderbilt as their sponsor. Known as the "Bewitching Brokers," the scheming sibs managed to clear $700,000 in profits before Cornelius recalled certain preexisting family obligations and withdrew, taking his valuable insider information with him.

"While others argued the equality of woman and man, I proved it by successfully engaging in business," Woodhull bragged, and went on to found the radical journal *Woodhull & Claflin's Weekly*, publishing not only pro-sex and pro-suffrage pieces, but also the first English translation of Marx's *Communist Manifesto.* "Christ was a Communist of the strictest sort, and so am I, and of the most extreme kind," noted the $700,000 candidate.

Predictably enough, however, voters found Woodhull's aberrant sex life far more alarming than her inconsistent political views. "My judges preach against 'free love' openly, and practice it secretly," she complained, and instigated her own personal

The scandalous suffragist

"outing" campaign by penning an article about a well-known minister's adulterous affair. But the counterattack did more damage to her credibility than to that of the clergyman, and needless to say, she did not prevail over incumbent president Ulysses S. Grant in the election of 1872.

In fact, even had women been permitted to vote in that year, the racy radical would not have been able to cast a ballot on her own behalf. Woodhull celebrated election day in jail, held on charges of sending obscene material through the mails, and the era named for a famous Victoria was thereafter remembered, rightly or wrongly, as one of extreme decorum.

"I have an inalienable, constitutional, and natural right to love whom I may...[and] to change that love every day if I please!"
—VW

LUCY HAYES

✳ ✳

ONE COLD DRINK OF WATER

EIGHTEEN SEVENTY-SEVEN WAS NOT A VINTAGE YEAR for American tipplers. Though Carry Nation and her saloon-smashing hatchet hadn't yet been glimpsed on the sober new horizon, the anti-booze campaign of the Women's Christian Temperance Union was picking up serious steam. And in the White House, setting the tone for the entire nation, sat strict teetotaler Rutherford B. Hayes and stricter-still First Lady Lucy, a prim paragon who never swerved from the temperance vow she took as a child.

Guests familiar with the more fluid social style of Ulysses and Julia Grant, the mansion's previous occupants, did not give up their drinking privileges without protest. Once, during the first months of the Hayes administration, Secretary of State William Evarts prevailed upon "Lemonade Lucy" to take pity on two visiting Russian dukes, for whom dinner *sans* spirits, he insisted, "would be an annoyance, if not an affront." But Mrs. Hayes, the first president's wife to hold a college degree, was too smart to be tricked into serving alcohol on the pretense of following tradition. "It is true I shall violate a precedent," she noted dryly, "but I shall not violate the Constitution, which is all that, through my husband, I have taken the oath to obey."

And so, as the secretary of state had it, "water flowed like champagne" at Lucy's liquorless table, and topers learned to make alternative arrangements. According to some, Rutherford B. simply looked the other way when a sympathetic White House steward started spiking bibulous diners' refreshments with rum. But the president (who, unlike Lucy, abstained only in order to attract prohibitionists to the Republican party) denied the rumor. The truth, he insisted, was that alcohol *flavoring* was added to certain dishes to pacify—or possibly outrage—certain non-abstinent guests. In any event, a more reliable source of spirits was the nearby "Last Chance" saloon (or the "First Chance," as the flip side of the street sign read), whose proprietor must have been one of the first lady's biggest fans.

Please don't B.Y.O.B.

Oddly enough, Lucy (who, with her severely tailored gowns and her hair drawn back tightly in a bun, looked every inch the prude) wasn't always such a fuddy-duddy. An 1854 lecture by radical Lucy Stone loosened her up a bit on the subject of women's rights, and she once ventured that "violent measures" might be justified in the pursuit of social reform. But as the first lady matured, any latent feminism remained bottled up inside—much to the dismay of liberated women who hoped to find an ally in the White House—and suffragists soon matched social drinkers in their disapproval of the president's puritanical wife. Not even her most ardent foes, however, could have come up with the epithet that the unworldly Mrs. Hayes ironically provided for herself. "Four years," she wrote as her husband approached the end of his term in 1881, "is long enough for a woman like this one." For once, Lemonade Lucy and a thirsty nation found themselves entirely in agreement.

"I trust I am not a fanatic, but I do want my influence to be always in favor of temperance."
—LH

MARIA HALPIN

* *

GROVER'S PREGNANT PARAMOUR

THOUGH PRESIDENT-TO-BE GROVER CLEVELAND found gal pal Maria Halpin a stimulating playmate, the Buffalo widow never had a prayer of waking up in the White House. A nation that even now has a hard time handling a first lady's new hairdo, after all, wasn't likely in the 1880s to warm up to a tippling bedhopper—much less the unabashed mother of an out-of-wedlock child.

But if a blatantly flawed female couldn't worm her way into the White House, she could certainly exert a powerful force to keep a man out—a fact which nearly cost bachelor candidate Cleveland the presidency in 1884. In fact, the entire election campaign that year centered around Cleveland's dalliance with Halpin, a popular party girl whom he had dated—and possibly impregnated—nearly a decade earlier.

"A Terrible Tale—Dark Chapter in Public Man's History," screamed the *Buffalo Evening Telegraph* when news of the shocking affair surfaced during the campaign. But the Democratic candidate didn't deny a thing—he simply gave the scandal his own special spin. According to his rather imaginative version of the story, Cleveland certainly didn't consider himself the only potential father of Halpin's son. Apparently, however, he did consider himself something of a saint: as the only unmarried man on intimate terms with the merry widow in 1874, he had selflessly agreed to support the child so that no otherwise-committed beaux would find themselves in an embarrassing position.

That, however, was just the beginning of the future president's long and tangled involvement with Halpin, whose propensity to party a bit too heartily was in no way modified by the birth of baby Oscar Cleveland. Once again, or so his line went, Cleveland did the right thing, obtaining a court order to remove his putative son from hard-drinking Halpin and place him in an orphanage. She countered by kidnapping the child, the orphanage retrieved him, and so it went for some time, until little Oscar was finally adopted by a prominent New York family, and Halpin left town with $500 of good-bye money from Cleveland in her pocket. Remarkably enough (attention, Gary Hart!), Cleveland's brazen tell-all tactic succeeded in stealing the fire from scandal-mongering opponent James Blaine, and rendered redundant any Republican efforts to dig the same dirt twice. A popular 1884 campaign slogan told the whole story: "Ma, Ma, where's my Pa? Gone to the White House, Ha, Ha, Ha!" Where, it might be added, "Pa" was quick to protect his recently rescued reputation by getting himself hitched to the virginal Frances ("Frank") Folsom, a twenty-one-year-old teetotaler whose character was entirely beyond reproach.

> *"I have my heart set upon making Frank a sensible,*
> *domestic American wife..."*
> —Grover Cleveland

A TRIVIAL NOTE

Few concerned citizens, one imagines, stay awake nights wondering why the Marine Band strikes up "Hail to the Chief" when the president makes a public appearance. But among our ever-inquisitive historians, it seems, a mini-controversy rages. One scholar credits First Lady Julia Tyler, the giddy June bride who enlivened husband John's White House from 1844 to 1845, with introducing that curious custom. A second school of thought, however, holds that Sarah Polk, Julia's immediate successor, implemented the institution to draw attention to diminutive spouse James, who didn't exactly stand out in the crowd. Whichever nineteenth-century innovator we have to thank or blame, however, there's only one real reason that the president still gets "Hailed" today: it's an American tradition.

SHARP-SHOOTER IN THE WHITE HOUSE

According to the once-startling assertion of Frances Benjamin Johnston, the nation's foremost female photographer at the turn of the century, women were ideally suited to a career behind the camera. Or so the Washington-based shutterbug, known both for her bohemian lifestyle and her candid commissioned portraits of Presidents B. Harrison, Cleveland, McKinley, T. Roosevelt, Taft, and their kin, claimed in her 1897 *Ladies Home Journal* article, "What A Woman Can Do With A Camera!" As a confirmed bachelorette romanced exclusively (so far, anyway, as the record shows) by one of her female colleagues, Johnston was living proof of another thing a lady photographer could do with her lens: gain access to fame and power without having to marry a man.

AND ON THE SEVENTH DAY, ALICE RESTED

Alice Roosevelt Longworth, a student of sorcery since childhood, didn't need any help negotiating in supernatural territory, thank you very much. Incensed that Papa Teddy had to vacate the White House in 1909 in deference to William Taft and his wife, TR's twenty-five-year-old daughter buried a voodoo doll on the grounds and pronounced a curse on the incoming residents. And indeed, a severe blizzard cast a symbolic pall over the first day of the Taft administration; nearly as noteworthy, the new first lady never got to flaunt her inaugural ball gown, which was trapped aboard a snowbound train. Not noted for undue modesty, the deliciously malicious Mrs. Longworth probably never doubted that her own occult handiwork—and not, for example, the impersonal forces of nature—conjured up the show-stopping storm.

ROSE CLEVELAND

✶ ✶

THE SUBLIMATING SISTER

ORED TO TEARS BY TEAS AND POLITE TÊTE-À-TÊTES, Rose Elizabeth Cleveland—the brainy, significantly single bluestocking who served a year-and-a-half stint as first hostess for big brother Grover—often amused herself by secretly meditating on Greek grammar while greeting White House guests.

Who knows—perhaps those stultifying state soirees might have taken a livelier turn had Rose not decreed that booze was banned in the presidential home. As it was, however, the ennui-ridden teetotaler impressed one visitor as "a little grim"; another found her "purposeful movements rather terrifying." But even without benefit of imbibing, many guests left the White House in a discombobulated state, thanks to one of Ms. Cleveland's stern lectures on the subject of women's suffrage.

No one who met her would argue that radical Rose—a college instructor, a seasoned public speaker, and the author of a scholarly tome titled *The Poetry of George Eliot and Other Subjects*—was the most conventional hostess ever to chat up a congressman's wife, or discuss the Washington weather. Nonetheless, the press insisted on packaging her in traditional first lady terms: her "Spanish lace over black silk" gown made the front page of the *New York Times*; not so a rather indifferent review of her book, buried deep inside the paper, and damning in its faint praise of the work's "warm and womanly" tone.

No doubt President Cleveland was as relieved as his silk-clad sister when his 1886 White House wedding terminated her term as stand-in. Whatever else the public might whisper about his union with Frances Folsom, a winsome family friend just barely out of her teens, no one was likely to find her, in contrast to his opinionated sibling, the least bit "masculine in manner." Nor did the president hesitate to express his hope that First Lady Frances would never succumb to the egalitarian "notions" to which her sister-in-law so heartily subscribed. "A good wife," he maintained was "a woman who loves her husband and her country with no desire to run either."

And indeed, White House social life would soon resume more classic contours under the surprisingly able direction of the president's quasi-child-bride. Meanwhile, finally free of the paralyzing public gaze, the woman whom guests found so grim plunged into an intensely romantic (and apparently quite delicious) private life, eventually taking up permanent residence in Italy with long-term lover Evangeline Simpson. Though Rose's passionate love letters enumerate various of Ms. Simpson's fine qualities (both physical and otherwise), chief among her charms seems to have been the ability to transport the former first hostess "to the summit of joy, the end of search, the goal of love!"— and far, far from the fearsome White House.

> *"[Women] can do no better or braver thing than to*
> *bring our best thoughts to the everyday market;*
> *they will yield us usurious interest."*
> —RC

FRANCES CLEVELAND

★ ★

TRIUMPH OF THE TROPHY WIFE

TIMES HAVE CERTAINLY CHANGED. When forty-nine-year-old President Grover Cleveland wed a twenty-one-year-old woman who was, in effect, his ward, nobody got her bustle in a bunch, or called for the smelling salts. In fact, Cleveland's June 1886 marriage to Frances "Frank" Folsom, the daughter of his deceased law partner, may well have been, as the *New York Mail and Express* asserted, "altogether the most popular act of [his] administration."

Never mind that the doting surrogate daddy who bought little Frances her first baby carriage was the same man who slipped the wedding ring on her finger. In 1886, no official couple had inhabited the White House for five years, and a romance-starved populace would, it seems, have applauded Cleveland's union with any woman who wasn't actually named the Whore of Babylon. The fact that Frances, a brand-new college grad, came across as graceful and mature (also, she had a cute hairstyle, and soon half the women in America had it too) was just the frosting on the wedding cake.

Of course, if Cleveland's bosomy (a detail overlooked by few historians) bride had known a few more tricks than the typical twenty-one-year-old of her day, it wouldn't have been a secret for long. From the moment the newlyweds said "I do," reporters pursued the pair relentlessly, even employing telescopes to keep tabs on the action during their Maryland honeymoon. So persistently were they hounded, in fact, that the Clevelands eventually sought refuge in a secluded private residence, inhabiting the White House only during the social season.

In matters that concerned the public and not the press, however, Frances took pains to remain accessible to her admirers. Defying advisors who shuddered at the prospect of "a rabble of shop girls" swarming around the first lady, she even added an extra weekly reception to her schedule, setting it for Saturday afternoons so that working women would have the opportunity to call. Thanks in part to perpetual media buzz, and in part to her own low-key charisma, Frances would eventually rank second only to Dolley Madison as the most popular first lady of the century, with "Frankie Cleveland" fan clubs sprouting up from coast to coast, and devotees slavishly copying her clothes, her coiffure, and even, when they posed for photographs, her posture.

A firm subscriber to the theory that only a tramp tells all, Frances never once granted an interview, or even wrote her memoirs. She and she alone knew her true feelings about her overnight ascent from obscurity to national obsession, or about the famous family friend who monopolized her affections from the moment she was old enough (one hopes) to have them. Eventually, however, even this endlessly fascinating first lady got her crack at a less scrutinized sort of life. Only forty-four at the time of Cleveland's death in 1908, she soon went on to enjoy a second honeymoon with an archaeologist of her own age—an event that was, happily, of far more interest to the principals than to the general public.

"She'll do."
—Grover Cleveland on the subject of First Lady Frances

BELVA LOCKWOOD

★ ★

PRECEDENTIAL MATERIAL

IN 1874, WHEN FORTY-FOUR-YEAR-OLD Belva Lockwood was denied permission to practice before the U.S. Court of Claims, the august Justice Drake found it necessary to explain the facts of life to her. "Mistress Lockwood, you are a woman," he pointed out. It was not the first time that the Washington, D.C. attorney had been apprised of that interesting bit of information: three years previously, several law schools had rejected her application on that basis, one noting that "the attendance of ladies would be an injurious diversion of the attention of the students."

It was, however, the first occasion on which the United States found itself sued by a female lawyer who, despite the "amazement and dismay" of "nine gowned judges," planned to practice law in the highest courts in the nation. And in 1879, after a fierce five-year battle with Congress to pass a bill guaranteeing that no citizen would "be excluded as attorney...from any court of the United States on account of sex," the persistent plaintiff became the first woman sworn in by both the Supreme Court and the Court of Claims. Not content to rest on her legal laurels, Ms. Lockwood went on to stun Washington by opening a mother-daughter law firm, successfully sponsoring the petition of the first black Southerner to practice before the Supreme Court, and winning a five-million-dollar settlement against the government for the Cherokee Nation.

By 1884, bold Belva's gender had apparently slipped her mind once again, and she announced herself as a candidate for the U.S. presidency on the ticket of the tiny National Equal Rights party. An anomaly in every way, the Lockwood presidential package included not only a platform calling for equal rights and "universal peace," but also would-be V.P. Marietta Stow, founder of a much-ridiculed California health regime known as "Cold Food." Nonetheless, the pair professed astonishing confidence in their popularity. "The Nation's heart beats in unison with the Equal-Rights party," opined optimistic Stow. Besides, she pointed out, a fifty-four-year-old female (unlike Democratic candidate Grover Cleveland, whose amorous indiscretions were then the subject of a raging national controversy) would certainly "bring no blush or barnacles of...'wild oats sowing' into the White House."

As it turned out, the Nation's heart was already smitten by Cleveland, his agricultural background notwithstanding, and did not consider Lockwood a serious rival for its

Litigious Lockwood

affections. Nor did the controversial candidate ever gain the full support of her feminist peers. "The damage done by her and a little band of eccentric zealots in California," sniffed one suffragist journal, "cannot be estimated." And, some suggested, the sole purpose of Lockwood's bid for office was to attract attention to herself, thereby increasing her law practice.

But Lockwood—who did manage to garner 4,149 votes (all of them cast, in that pre-Nineteenth Amendment year, by members of the opposite sex), and the entire electoral vote of Indiana—never regretted her decision, and went on to repeat the experiment, though with less success, in 1888. "We shall never have rights until we take them, or respect until we command it," she wrote. And, she added, for once not waiting for someone else to bring up the subject of her sex: "My cause was the cause of thousands of women."

"Reforms are slow, but they never go backward."
—BL

R.S.V.P. AT YOUR OWN RISK

★ ★

ALSO, DON'T POLISH YOUR TEETH WITH THE TABLECLOTH

ETIQUETTE AS OBSERVED IN EUROPEAN COURTS is not known at the White House," noted Hugo Ziemann, Steward of the White House, in 1887. Evidently not: judging by the topics treated in the so-called *White House Cookbook*—an eclectic guide to proper deportment, favorite state dinner menus, and effective deworming techniques, authored by Ziemann and one Mrs. F. L. Gillette—those nineteenth-century White House denizens and their pals were quite an uncouth lot.

Which greedy gourmand of a first lady, one wonders, inspired the admonition that "to take her teeth to [a bone] gives a lady the look of caring a little too much for the pleasures of the table"? Which dainty fashion plate provoked a diatribe against diners with "an affected way of holding the knife halfway down its length, as if it were too big for their little hands"? And was it some frustrated former acrobat, never fully resigned to her dull station in life, who breached the cardinal rule of beverage consumption: "Don't, when you drink, elevate your glass as if you were going to stand it inverted on your nose"?

It's too late now, of course, for those bone-picking, wobbly-wristed, wine-guzzling women—whoever they may have been—to make amends for their ill-bred ways. Should the modern-day student of etiquette, however, someday find herself dining *en famille* with the First Family (well, it *could* happen), there is absolutely no excuse for failing to "keep the mouth closely shut while masticating the food"—though not necessarily, as Ziemann and Gillette would probably have it, at every other moment as well.

"There is no position where the innate refinement of a person is more fully exhibited than at the table..."

—HZ

THE TOAST OF HER TABLE

No doubt a less self-assured young woman would have been daunted by stepping into the queen-sized shoes of an Abigail Adams or a Dolley Madison. But not so twenty-five-year-old Priscilla Cooper Tyler, who confidently served as White House hostess in the early 1840s when her bed-bound mother-in-law, Letitia Tyler, was unable to fill the position. After all, explained the erstwhile (and evidently rather experienced) actress, "I am considered *'charmante'* by the Frenchmen, 'lovely' by the Americans and 'really quite nice, you know' by the English." Needless to say, the adorable Priscilla was also considered quite the bee's knees by herself.

EDITH ROOSEVELT

✸ ✸

THE DEMURE DICTATOR

A LADY'S NAME," OPINED FIRST LADY Edith Roosevelt, "should appear in print only three times: at her birth, marriage, and death." Needless to say, any modern-day president's spouse who tried to enforce such a quaint P.R. policy would find herself laughed right out of Lincoln's bedroom. But even in 1901, when Edith and Theodore set up housekeeping at 1600 Pennsylvania, the affairs of the first family were deemed the affairs of the nation. And with six rambunctious offspring in tow (among them TR's daughter from his first marriage, the aberrant, attention-loving Alice), the Republican Roosevelts would probably have drawn a crowd at the circus.

Determined to maintain maximum decorum, however, Edith developed her own techniques for managing the press. Major publications were kept well-stocked with posed photos of herself and her brood, thereby warding off the intrusion of paparazzi, and no doubt making for more flattering shots. And after one national rag noted that the first lady (who scrimped to feed her family of eight on the president's salary) "dresses on 300 dollars a year and looks it," she continued to model the same ensemble evening after evening—while ordering reporters to describe gowns of varying hues.

But the press wasn't the only institution over which old-fashioned Edith exercised iron control. In stark contrast to Julia Grant, who had, a quarter of a century earlier, thrown the White House doors open to all, Edith decreed that ladies who wished to attend her receptions must formally apply for the privilege. Dismayed to discover that capital streetwalkers made a game of trying to sneak into the White House, she scrutinized guest lists with an especially ruthless eye. Though history fails to indicate whether any tainted doves were routed, the record does reveal that black women, slum dwellers, and the non-monogamous Grand Duke Boris of Russia all failed to make the grade. And on one occasion, the moral arbiter in the White House informed an alleged adulteress that she would no longer be welcome in Washington unless she mended her errant ways.

The pillar of propriety

Not even the president, in fact, was exempt from uptight Edith's dictates. At her insistence, he saw his adored sisters only by appointment, and meekly accepted his daily twenty-dollar allowance directly from his wife's hand. "Now remember to be good while I'm away," she sometimes commanded, as though Teddy were merely another of her children. And when he contemplated running for a third term in 1912, his spouse promptly disabused him of the notion. "Put it out of your mind," she ordered, "You will never be president again"—and, of course, he wasn't.

Just as Edith would have deemed proper, the many macho exploits of her husband—trustbuster, big-game hunter, and rough-riding Spanish-American War hero—would one day figure prominently in the pages of American history texts, with nary a word about herself. To a woman of her genteel Victorian sensibility, it simply went without saying that men weren't the only ones who knew the value of speaking softly...or carrying the proverbial big stick.

"One hates to feel that all one's life is public property."
—ER

ALICE ROOSEVELT LONGWORTH

✫ ✫

A NATIONAL INSTITUTION

"I CAN DO ONE OF TWO THINGS," protested Theodore Roosevelt when a friend wondered why he didn't take a stricter line with his daughter Alice, just seventeen and already notoriously sassy when Teddy took office in 1901. "I can be President of the United States, or I can control Alice. I cannot possibly do both."

As Alice's news-making antics throughout TR's two terms in office made clear, her father obviously took the easier path. The oldest and by far the most outrageous of the six Roosevelt siblings, she surreptitiously sipped cocktails, placed wagers at the racetrack, and often unnerved state visitors by introducing them to Emily Spinach, a slithery green pet snake. On a trip to San Francisco in 1905, she took along a revolver and amused herself by plugging the passing telegraph poles from her seat on a moving train. And when reporters pressed for details of what the president's daughter would be wearing at a particular dinner or ball, she regaled them with vivid, utterly fictitious descriptions of costly velvet and satin ensembles that she didn't actually own.

When Teddy discovered that his wild child had taken up the nasty vice of smoking, he forbade her to use tobacco inside his home. Thereafter, agile Alice puffed in good conscience atop the White House roof, in perfect accordance with the letter, if not the spirit, of the law. And that wasn't (or so the newspapers noted) nearly all: she plunged fully clothed into swimming pools, stripped to her skivvies at a party, and most audaciously of all, went driving with Nicholas Longworth—a middle-aged Ohio congressman headed toward a career as speaker of the house—without benefit of a chaperone. If naughty "Princess Alice" (as she was known to the press) and her escort were not engaged, opined the old-fashioned reporter who scooped that red-hot story, they certainly "ought to be."

Fortunately for all concerned (and clearly, many were), Alice's fabled East Room wedding to Mr. Longworth in 1906 failed to transform the president's prankish daughter into a staid Washington matron. Irrepressible as ever, the madcap Mrs. L. cultivated a passion for playing poker with the boys, concocted bathtub gin in her basement, deliberately seated sworn enemies together at her famous dinner parties, and reportedly tangled with crusader Carry Nation on the subject of her smoking. "They expect me to wear a halo and I only wear a hat," smirked Alice, who, truth be told, quite enjoyed the attention (and whose outsize headgear, as it happened, often concealed a flask of bootleg hootch). And long after Theodore Roosevelt's death in 1919, she remained such a prominent fixture in capital culture that wags eventually took to calling her "Washington's Other Monument."

Needless to say, Alice's extended old age—throughout which she prided herself on wangling "2.7 dinners a year in the White House no matter who is president"—was scarcely a dull affair. At the advanced age of ninety, she astounded all observers at a D.C. party by twisting her still-limber limbs into a full-lotus position, then wrapping a live boa constrictor around her neck. "I'm just one of the show-off Roosevelts," shrugged Teddy's still-uncontrollable daughter as the other guests stood gaping. "I just perform." And, she noted smugly, "I give a good show."

"Fill what's empty, empty what's full, and scratch where it itches."
—ARL

THE WICKED WIT OF
ALICE ROOSEVELT LONGWORTH

"If I err, it will not be on the side of the angels," Alice Roosevelt Long-worth once observed. Not that the sharp-eyed Washington socialite, who saw eighteen presidential administrations come and go during her ninety-six years of life, was ever far off the mark. But it was true that her tart tongue seemed more diabolically than divinely inspired. Among the prominent victims of Alice's biting barbs:

THEODORE ROOSEVELT (HER FATHER):

"Father always wants to be the corpse at every funeral, the bride at every wedding, and the baby at every christening."

WILLIAM TAFT:

"He has so much brain and so little beauty!"

WARREN HARDING:

"Saying that Harding is second rate is one of the biggest compliments anyone can pay him."

CALVIN COOLIDGE:

"Coolidge looks like he was weaned on a pickle."

HERBERT HOOVER:

"The Hoover Vacuum Cleaner is more exciting than the president. But, of course, it's electric!"

ELEANOR ROOSEVELT (HER COUSIN):

"A great dear but a very boring dear!"

THOMAS DEWEY (TWO-TIME GOP PRESIDENTIAL CANDIDATE):

"How do you expect people to vote for a man who looks like a bridegroom on a wedding cake?"

JACQUELINE KENNEDY ONASSIS:

"Hasn't anyone ever warned Jacqueline Kennedy about Greeks bearing gifts?"

LYNDON JOHNSON (WHO PROUDLY FLAUNTED AN ABDOMINAL SURGICAL SCAR):

"Thank God it wasn't his prostate!"

AND HERSELF:

"The secret of eternal youth is arrested development."

ANOTHER ROOSEVELT RETORTS

Even in the White House, devoted bro Teddy relied (a tad too much, according to his second wife) on the advice of female sibs Bye and Corrine. Fortunately, he didn't also depend on their diplomatic skills. On one occasion, Corrine mentioned her brother to a casual acquaintance she happened to encounter on a train. "Oh, yes. Your brother," murmured her companion, who, truth be told, seemed to be having some trouble placing Corrine's face. "What is he doing now?"

"Oh, he's still president of the United States," deadpanned Theodore Roosevelt's sassy little sis.

HELEN TAFT

★ ★

BIG WILL'S BACKSEAT DRIVER

IN 1883, TWENTY-TWO-YEAR-OLD HELEN "Nellie" Herron (soon to be Mrs. William Taft) launched a weekly salon to engage in "brilliant discussion of topics intellectual" in her hometown of Cincinnati. "We were bent on improving our minds," the Madame de Staël of the Midwest—who wasn't too sophisticated to enjoy the occasional cigarette or stein of beer—would later recall. Molding minds, however, wasn't all that brainy Nell, the daughter of one congressman and granddaughter of another, was bent on. At the age of seventeen, it seems, a brief White House visit to family friends Rutherford and Lucy Hayes had infused her with a unique ambition: to become first lady of the United States.

Unfortunately, Nellie's handpicked ticket to the top, salon member William Taft, didn't harbor any secret desire to head the nation. Indeed, placid Will was little inclined to abandon the legal field for any reason. "Politics is sick," the future president of the United States once remarked. But Nellie, whom Will wed in 1886, *would* have her way. In 1901, when President McKinley tapped the dubious Mr. Taft to establish the first American governorship of the Philippines it was Mrs. Taft who insisted the family pack its bags for an exotic four-year exercise in career building. (It was also Mrs. Taft who got a kick out of surfing on Hawaii's Waikiki Beach *en route*.) In 1906, when President Theodore Roosevelt dangled a Supreme Court appointment before the drooling Will, Nellie personally intervened to make Teddy withdraw the offer—her goal, after all, was not to be a mere U.S. justice's wife. And in 1908, her worn-down spouse finally agreed to throw his hat in the ring, albeit without any great show of grace. "I was engaged in the respectable business of trying to administer justice [but] I have fallen from that state now," grumbled the reluctant (though ultimately successful) candidate.

On Inaugural Day in 1909, Nellie's triumph was complete, and the new first lady celebrated her victory by boldly accompanying her husband to the White House in the presidential carriage (hitherto, spouses had modestly trailed behind). "Of course there was objection," she wrote, but "in spite of protests [I] took my place at my husband's side." Nellie never did get a chance to savor her glory, however—just two months later, she suffered a debilitating stroke, and was forced to abandon her long-sought role as the nation's chief spousal supervisor. Ironically, her one visible accomplishment as first lady— adorning the capital with thousands of flowering cherry trees—proved to be of a totally traditional nature. And in the end, it was wishy-washy Will who went down in history as a great precedent setter, becoming, in 1921, the only former U.S. president to serve, as he had so long desired, as chief justice of the Supreme Court.

"Don't sit up nights thinking about making me president. I have no ambition in that direction."
—William Taft

LOW PROFILE, HIGH IMPACT

BEHIND-THE-SCENES LADY BOUNTIFULS

ELEANOR ROOSEVELT, AS EVERY SCHOOLGIRL KNOWS (or should), collected causes like Imelda Marcos stockpiled shoes; Jackie Kennedy spruced up the presidential digs until she was blue in the face and her status as aesthetic standard-bearer assured. But lesser-known first ladies, too, did their bit to make the world—or at least the White House—a more pleasant place to live...

IN 1818, A FUTURE FIRST COUPLE met cute when eighteen-year-old Millard Fillmore became a student at the New York State schoolhouse over which nineteen-year-old Abigail presided. Though ambitious Millard soon moved on to practice law, dear Abby (who wed her pupil the following year) never did lose her schoolmarm ways. When she and Mill finally made it to the White House in 1850, the bookish first lady refused to accept any social invitations whatsoever, opting instead to lock herself away in the library. Of course, there *wasn't* any library in the president's residence until Abigail sent Millard off to Congress to request funds to establish one.

✶ ✶ ✶

IN THE EARLY 1890s, CLEAN-FREAK Caroline Harrison distinguished herself from previous first ladies, in the eyes of her contemporaries, as "the best housekeeper the White House has ever known." During her industrious three-year residency (Caroline succumbed to tuberculosis before husband Benjamin completed his term), she renovated the kitchen, installed a more modern heating system, and saw that each bedroom was outfitted with a private bath. (Those nifty new W.C.s, bragged Ben, "would tempt a duck to wash himself every day.") In the course of her career as domestic goddess, Caroline also decorated the first White House Christmas tree and assembled the core of the historic presidential china collection that still fascinates tourists today. Her most shocking accomplishment by far, however, was to electrify the White House in 1891, bringing the then-nonagenarian mansion almost all the way into the twentieth century.

⋆　⋆　⋆

ELLEN WILSON, WOODROW'S NO. 1 WIFE, didn't rest on her laurels after becoming first lady in 1913. Appalled by living conditions in the capital's largely black slums, she persuaded members of Congress to sponsor the so-called Alley Dwelling bill to upgrade housing for the poor. The proposed piece of legislation languished on the back burner, however, until she became terminally ill the following year, and the Senate rushed to push it through before her death. Satisfied with her accomplishment, Ellen rested in peace in August 1914. So, incidentally, did the city's female civil servants, who, thanks to the first lady's *other* pet project, finally acquired restroom facilities of their own.

III

FROM WAR TO WAR:
A RISING FEMINIST UPROAR

EDITH WILSON

★★★★★★★★★★★★★★★★★★★★★★★★

WOODROW'S SEXY SURROGATE

FOND OF CHIC COUTURE AND ZIPPING AROUND Washington at the wheel of her own motorcar, wealthy widow Edith Galt was accustomed to making quite a splash. Even the worldly first lady-to-be, however, couldn't have anticipated the tizzy touched off by her romance with President Woodrow Wilson, a widower of only seven months in the summer of 1914 when he first succumbed to her womanly charms.

"What did Mrs. Galt do when the President asked her to marry him?" asked Washington wags, eager as always to spread news of a budding White House scandal. "She fell out of bed!" And when the *Washington Post* asserted that "The President spent much of the evening entering Mrs. Galt," many maintained that the typo (in fact, the reporter only observed the head of state *entertaining* his lady friend) was more credible than the correction.

Even the Mrs. Grundys of the nation couldn't deny, however, that Woodrow's second bride did much to lift his spirits during the anguishing crises of World War I. But contrary to innuendo, the bulk of Edith's patriotic services were not performed in the privacy of the bedroom. "Much as I enjoy your delicious love letters," she wrote to the president before their December 1915 marriage, "I enjoy even more the ones in which you tell me...of what you are working on." Once installed in the White House, the new first lady rapidly made her husband's business her own, finding it far more fascinating, for example, to decode classified military messages for him than to throw the *de rigueur* dinner parties. And in 1919, when the two-term president traveled to Paris to pitch his postwar League of Nations plan, Edith tagged along too, hiding behind a heavy curtain to listen in on her husband's secret negotiations with European treaty makers.

Not until Woodrow suffered a half-paralyzing stroke later that year, however, did the omnipresent first lady seriously outrage Washington politicians, barring their access to the bedridden president and substituting herself as his proxy at top-level meetings. "The only decision that was mine was what was important [to communicate to the president] and what was not," Edith would later write. But skeptical congressmen weren't certain that their views ever reached his ears, especially when they noted that the president's signature on certain documents bore a striking resemblance to that of his spouse. Mrs. Wilson, seethed one Republican senator, was a "presidentress who had fulfilled the dream of the suffragettes by changing her title from First Lady to Acting First Man." And while Edith spoke lightly of her eighteen-month "stewardship," others termed it "Petticoat Government," and even the "Mrs. Wilson regency."

Evidently the Acting First Man wasn't quite as power-hungry as her critics claimed, however—when a semi-recovered Woodrow suggested he might run for another term in 1920, she promptly vetoed the plan. Nor, it appears, did the tenure of the former sex object as presidential stand-in prove too ruinous to bear potential repetition: not until 1967 did Congress get around to ratifying the Twenty-Fifth Constitutional Amendment, specifically stating that the vice president of the United States (and not merely an enthusiastic volunteer) would assume the reins of power if ever again a president were disabled.

> *"Of course the burning question was how best to serve the*
> *country—and yet protect the President."*
> —EW

FLORENCE HARDING

✮ ✮

WARREN'S ORIGINAL WOMAN

WELL, WARREN, I HAVE GOT YOU THE PRESIDENCY; what are you going to do with it?" So Florence Harding—who pushed her senator spouse to run for top office in 1920, relentlessly pursued that new phenomenon known as the women's vote, and barked that he was going to run until "hell freezes over" when Warren tried to bow out along the way—inquired of her newly inaugurated husband in 1921.

In fact, handsome, henpecked Warren, who proved to be one of the weakest leaders in U.S. history, never did come up with a satisfactory answer to Flo's question. Though wildly popular at the outset of his administration, the Ohioan whose chief political idea was a return to something called "normalcy" spent most of his presidential days shuffling ineffectually through the papers on his desk, and his nights playing poker and swilling bathtub hooch.

Sixty-year-old Florence (five years her husband's senior, and according to her, his intellectual superior as well), on the other hand, knew just how to handle her hard-won stint in the White House. First of all, she would hire a Secret Service agent to tail her chronically unfaithful spouse, and order him to escort her astrologer, Madame Marcia (who had predicted both Harding's victory and his death in office), to and from the White House on the side. She'd personally mix the drinks for Warren's private card parties (booze provided, Prohibition notwithstanding, by a bootlegging buddy of hers)—then dash downstairs to preside over *official* (and officially dry) White House receptions.

And, of course, the "Duchess" (as Warren rather pointedly referred to her) would also continue to act as her husband's closest advisor, sometimes writing, sometimes editing his speeches, and, on the rare occasions when he felt compelled to make a decision, informing him of what he thought. "I know what's best for the President," she insisted. "I put him in the White House. He does well when he listens to me and poorly when he does not."

Inevitably, of course, stories circulated about the skewed balance of power chez Harding—his automobile, Warren himself joked, was the only thing he possessed that his wife "did not have a desire to run." And when, just as Madame Marcia had predicted, the president expired suddenly in August 1923, rumors raged that it was Florence, bent on shielding him from the humiliation of the breaking Teapot Dome scandal and

Smarter than her spouse

other intimations of deep Cabinet corruption, who actually did him in. Whether or not the Duchess (who, curiously, refused to allow an autopsy) contributed to her husband's death, however, no one will ever know. After torching as many of his presidential papers as she could get her hands on, she followed Warren to the grave a year later, apparently unwilling to allow even death to thwart her eternal scrutiny.

> *"Mrs. Harding wants to be the drum major in*
> *every band that passes."*
> —Mr. Harding

NAN BRITTON

✶ ✶

WARREN'S OTHER WOMAN

AS WARREN HARDING'S FATHER LIKED TO SAY, it was a good thing his son wasn't a member of the opposite sex, or the twenty-ninth president of the United States would have constantly been "in the family way" due to his well-known inability to say no. Still, it takes two to do the hokey-pokey, and in Warren's case, willing women were scarcely in short supply. Decidedly the willingest, however, was young Nan Britton, who first set her sights on Warren when she was a high school freshman in 1910.

Initially, Miss Britton expressed her infatuation with her fellow Marion, Ohio resident—then and always some thirty years her senior—by writing "I love Warren Harding" on the blackboard and mooning over his congressional campaign posters. Not until 1917, however, when Nan was attending secretarial school in New York, did she initiate correspondence with the sexy (but decidedly not single) senator on the seemingly innocuous subject of how to find a job. Warren promptly secured her a post as a stenographer for the U.S. Steel Corporation, and, when he next visited New York, was personally rewarded with a somewhat more substantial gesture than a thank-you note. Soon Nan was regularly sharing "love's sweetest intimacy," as she delicately phrased it, with her long-coveted man. By 1919, she was also sharing the news that she and Warren had conceived a child on the couch of his Senate office in January of that year.

Evidently Warren, elected president in 1920, managed to keep the fact of his extramarital fatherhood a secret from his spouse, Florence. Nothing, however, could prevent the ever-vigilant first lady from detecting the affair, which her husband continued to carry on right under her nose (and, often, in a five-by-five closet in the Oval Office) for several years. Indeed, a slew of Secret

Service agents presided over the none-too-subtle dalliance, most charged with standing guard outside one closed door or another, and one assigned by Mrs. Harding (with predictably dramatic results) to find out exactly what was going on within.

Those amusing White House escapades were to cease, of course, with the president's sudden death in August of 1923. Not so, however, Nan's grand passion, preserved in all its lurid splendor in her best-selling 1927 memoir, *The President's Daughter*—a double-edged literary coup that not only revealed one of the darkest secrets in Warren Harding's crowded closet, but provided the author with the means to support his child for quite some time.

> *"I don't think there are any men who are faithful to their wives."*
> —Jacqueline Kennedy

WHY BEAUTIFUL MOVIE STARS ARE A THREAT TO NATIONAL SECURITY

Not only did Calvin Coolidge seldom speak, but as president during Prohibition in the 1920s, he also didn't drink. Not, that is, until actress Marion Davies, the infamous mistress of William Randolph Hearst and his castle, slyly served him a glass of sweet wine and passed it off as fruit juice. When the first glass went down with ease, the thirsty teetotaler took a second shot of the supposedly innocuous beverage, and eventually requested a third. Lo and behold, three glasses of liquor rendered close-mouthed Calvin relatively loquacious. "I don't know when I've had anything as refreshing," he gushed to his secretly smirking hostess.

THE HAND THAT ROCKED THE CRADLE (AND RAISED THE RAFTERS)

Like most mothers of her day, Janet "Jessie" Wilson apparently thought it her obligation to make a lovely home for her family. And so, in 1871, she did, personally drawing up plans for an elegant South Carolina mansion surrounded by magnolias, and supervising the construction herself. Thanks to his female parent's foresight, son Woodrow was quite accustomed to splendid surroundings by the time he took up residence in the White House, and probably didn't have to adjust much—architecturally speaking—to the office at all.

LET THEM DRINK TEA

Though many historians rank Woodrow Wilson as one of the greatest American presidents, the recipient of the 1919 Nobel Peace Prize never won any popularity contests among members of the women's suffrage movement. On one occasion, a delegation of protesters stormed the sidewalk outside the White House carrying a streamer that read, in part, "We, the women of America, tell you that America is not a democracy... Twenty million American women are denied the right to vote." Watching from the window, the president wasn't moved by their message, but he was concerned for their welfare: the weather was chilly, and so Wilson dispatched a member of his staff to invite the ladies in for a cup of tea.

Though the president's intentions were chivalrous rather than callous, tea was not the type of concession the picketers had in mind, and the invitation was rejected out of hand. Eventually, several suffragists were arrested for disturbing the peace and sentenced to short jail terms, and Wilson went on to achieve his prominent place in history largely on the strength of his efforts to establish the League of Nations—and not his support for the League of Women Voters.

BUT HE STILL KNEW HOW TO WHISTLE

Certainly Lauren Bacall didn't lack for big-name beaux—at one time or another, Kirk Douglas, Frank Sinatra, and, of course, Humphrey Bogart all double-billed with the husky-voiced Hollywoodite. But in 1945, the twenty-one-year-old *To Have and Have Not* star suddenly took it into her head to vamp then-V.P. Harry Truman. Visiting the National Press Club in Washington, Bacall waited until Harry (an avid recreational pianist) sat down at the Steinway, then slithered atop the piano and struck a luscious cheesecake pose. Naturally, Press Club reporters rushed to avail themselves of the not-quite-pornographic photo op, with the regrettable result that HST's better half soon decreed that it was time for her hubby to stop tickling the ivories in public.

CARRIE PHILLIPS

✶✶✶✶✶✶✶✶✶✶✶✶✶✶✶✶✶✶✶✶✶✶✶✶

ANOTHER OF WARREN'S WOMEN

A CCORDING TO WARREN HARDING'S WISE OLD MOM, her daughter-in-law Florence should make sure she kept the icebox well-stocked—and both her eyes on Warren. If Mom was right, we can only assume that the Harding marriage ran amok for reasons relating to an empty larder: not only did Florence keep her gaze glued to her run-around guy, but once the Hardings made it to the White House, she even hired an assistant to help her with the job. But in the end (and probably, one gathers, at the beginning), Warren was fiercely determined to stray.

So, it happened, was Carrie Phillips, the bored wife of Warren's dear old friend Jim, who the future president (then the lieutenant governor of Ohio) first romanced in 1905. Conveniently, both Mrs. Harding and Mr. Phillips suffered from chronic ailments, and with one spouse laid up with an ailing kidney and the other on the mend at a mental facility, Carrie allowed Warren (or was it the other way around?) to have his way. Apparently the encounter proved mutually gratifying, as the undercover affair smoldered on for years, even during the joint vacations to Europe and Bermuda that the two families enjoyed in 1909 and 1911.

When Carrie ceased to take the clandestine relationship casually, however, all hell broke loose—Warren refused to leave his wife, and Carrie ran off to Berlin in a fit of pique, probably leaving a very puzzled spouse behind. Still, when she returned home at the outbreak of World War I in 1914, the enthusiastic adulterers (one of whom was now officially addressed as "Senator") took up right where they left off. But before long, the capricious Mrs. Phillips and her secret paramour were once again on the outs. Thoroughly enamored of Berlin since her impromptu sojourn, Carrie didn't share Warren's hawkish views vis-à-vis Germany, and huffily informed her senator that she'd go public with their affair if he voted for the U.S. to enter the war. He ignored her threat; she ignored the insult; America joined the Allies, and, as usual, Carrie and Warren continued to carry on.

But unlike Nan Britton, Warren's other (and concurrent) long-term mistress, Carrie Phillips never had the opportunity to bed her honey in the White House. In 1920, when the Republican National Committee, which had just nominated Warren for president, finally caught wind of the affair, it packed the potentially troublesome Mr. and Mrs. Phillips off on a free junket to Japan faster than you could say "Donna Rice." Sad to say, though a profound political difference of opinion didn't succeed in separating Carrie from her man, a healthy infusion of Republican hush money did: a $20,000 lump sum and monthly payments for the rest of the president's term in office proved to be quite adequate to quench Carrie's libido—or, more to the point, securely seal her lips.

> *"I don't remember any love affairs.*
> *One must keep love affairs quiet."*
> —The Duchess of Windsor

GRACE COOLIDGE

✶ ✶

TOO HAPPY FOR HER HUSBAND

WHEN GRACE COOLIDGE FIRST LAID EYES on her spouse-to-be the summer of 1904, he was nattily clad in his B.V.D.s and a brown derby hat, and the incongruous sight, glimpsed through an open window, made Grace laugh out loud. But even after she got to know her nearly nude neighbor a little bit better (he wore the hat while shaving, he explained, to keep his hair out of his face), Calvin's mannerisms continued to crack her up. And the first time she heard him lecture in public, his rural Vermont accent sent Grace into such giggles that she had to duck behind a pillar while she tried to regain her composure.

But being married to the ambitious politician wasn't always a barrel of laughs—as the twenty-six-year-old sign language teacher, who said "I do" in 1905, had ample opportunity to find out. For one thing, her man didn't always manage to hold up his end of the conversation, a fact duly noted by Grace's dubious friends. "Having taught the deaf to hear, she may now inspire the dumb to speak," quipped one wag. Even eighteen years later, when laconic Cal was transformed overnight into President Coolidge, he remained uncommonly fond of the silent treatment. "I'm sorry for you," Grace cracked to one socialite who thought she'd stumbled into great good fortune when she was seated next to Calvin. "You'll have to do all the talking yourself."

But close-mouthed Calvin, who presided over the Oval Office from 1923 to 1929, didn't confine his conservatism to matters involving words. "I think you will find you will get along at this job fully as well, if you don't try anything new," he advised the first lady (far more passionate about athletic pursuits, and just about everything else, than he) when she expressed an interest in horseback riding. Also verboten, for the sake of her husband's dignified image: bobbing her hair, driving a car, dancing in public, engaging in political discussions, and wearing trousers for hiking in the country. "Being wife to a government worker is a very confining position," the president's wife confided to a friend.

Her husband's quaint concepts notwithstanding, Grace proved to be one of the most adept White House hostesses since the days of Dolley Madison—owing in part, one imagines, to all those years of trying to liven up (or even launch) discussions at home. One old-timer ventured her opinion that no woman had "ever wrung so much pleasure out of Washington or given so much in return," and even acerbic newsman Will Rogers dubbed the genial first lady "Public Female Favorite No. 1."

Converting Calvin to a less rigid point of view, however, was not among the numerous social coups scored by Grace, who went on to enjoy nearly another quarter-century of life after her husband's death in 1933. "Well, I thought I would get him to enjoy life and have fun," she admitted, "but he was not very easy to instruct in that way."

> *"I had my hands full discharging the duties of the position to which I had not been elected."*
> —GC

LOU HOOVER

★ ★

DOMESTIC DISASTER

"IT TAKES JUST AS MUCH COURAGE TO STICK to the housework until it is done as it does to go out and meet a bear," First Lady-to-be Lou Hoover told a Girl Scout convention in 1927. And in the case of hardy Mrs. Hoover—one of the grittiest presidential spouses ever to come down the pike—grappling with a grizzly was probably the preferable chore.

The first woman to graduate from Stanford University with a geology degree, Lou wed her classmate Herbert in 1899 and promptly set sail for Tientsin, China, where Herbie headed up a mining program—but not for long. Evidently more thrilled than terrified at being caught up in the Boxer Rebellion of 1900, adaptable Lou learned to live behind barricades, survived having her bicycle shot out from under her, and calmly dealt herself a game of solitaire while sniper fire peppered her backyard. In London during World War I, she enjoyed similarly stimulating adrenalin rushes, racing up to the roof to pinpoint exactly where German bombs were landing. (During more tranquil moments, Lou relaxed by translating a classic sixteenth-century Latin text on metallurgy.) And back in the States, she became such a passionate advocate of outdoor activities for women that Girl Scout founder Juliette Low personally recruited her to serve on the organization's national board.

Facing the rigors of first ladydom, however, required a different sort of pluck. Scarcely had Herbert Hoover taken office in 1929 than the stock market crashed, and the country plunged into the Great Depression; it was not, in short, an ideal time to test drive the occupation of president's wife (nor, of course, of president).

With unemployment rampant and desperate families driven from their homes, not all were equally cheered by Mrs. Hoover's buck-up radio speeches advocating volunteerism, and suggesting there was "ample food and clothing for us all" if only Americans would share. In 1930, the Southern section of the nation became further disillusioned with Lou when she dared to invite a black congressman's wife to tea in the White House. The *Mobile Alabama Press* led the attack, ranting that the first lady's "arrogant insult" had defiled the Executive Mansion, and the Texas legislature passed a resolution officially criticizing the act. Inspired by her example, however, the president promptly invited a black professor from Tuskegee College to join him at home for lunch.

A trouper to the bitter end, Lou continued to promote her husband's ever-less-popular policies, and was disappointed when voters did not return him to office in 1932, placing their confidence in FDR instead. But as she showed her successor, Eleanor Roosevelt, around the White House grounds, it became apparent that there was one challenge that even the indomitable Mrs. Hoover couldn't face. "I'm sorry, but the housekeeper will have to show you the kitchens," murmured the first lady whom neither violent revolutions nor falling bombs had managed to faze. "I never go into the kitchens."

"It isn't so important what others think of you
as what you feel inside."
—LH

ELEANOR ROOSEVELT

✸ ✸

A BRAND NEW DEAL

W HEN ELEANOR ROOSEVELT LEARNED on election day in 1932 that her husband was to be the next president of the United States, the tears she wept were not for joy. "Now I'll have no identity," she mourned.

Nothing, of course, could have been further from the truth. An activist icon whose very name triggered many a subsequent first lady's insecurity complex, Eleanor transcended a Victorian upbringing and her chronic self-doubt to challenge every preexisting notion of proper conduct for a president's spouse. One contemporary columnist spoke for millions when he termed her "the most influential woman of our times."

Uncertain at the time of her 1905 marriage, Eleanor later admitted, of the distinction between state and national legislature, the most admired first lady in history might never have expanded her horizons much beyond hearth and home. But spurred by anger over Franklin's extramarital affair in 1918, then by her decision to serve as his "eyes and ears" when polio left him paralyzed soon thereafter, she deliberately turned her back on tradition. The first presidential spouse to hold her own press conferences, to serve (as cochair of the Office of Civilian Defense) in an official government position, to write a syndicated column—the list goes on and on. Without regret, Eleanor left the pampering of her husband to more willing women during her twelve-year term as first lady. For her, there were other pressing concerns—among them the elimination of racism, sexism, and poverty.

While Franklin hammered out the policies of his Depression-busting New Deal, Eleanor roamed the country gathering data on the quality of American life, now showing up at a migrant workers' camp in California, now donning overalls to descend into the coal mines of Appalachia. "Mrs. Roosevelt Spends Night At The White House!" one tongue-in-cheek *Washington Post* headline read. "She is in prison, Mr. President," the first lady's secretary once informed FDR, who hadn't realized his wife was touring a Baltimore penitentiary. ("I'm not surprised," he replied, "but what for?") And at a conference in Alabama in 1939, "Eleanor Everywhere" finally managed to be in two places at once, symbolically seating herself smack in the middle of the aisle segregating black attendees from whites.

Chatting up a woman machinist

"Dear God, please make Eleanor a little tired," Franklin (who received an exhaustive report of each of those fact-finding journeys) was said to implore, but he never stopped relying on her advice. Anyway, the indefatigable first lady (who also wrote, lectured, and was bombarded by some 300,000 letters a year) had no apparent need for rest: even on New Year's Eve, her niece reported, she spared only a few minutes to share "a round of toasts," then worked until the small hours of the morning.

"The story is over," Eleanor told reporters as she left the White House after Franklin's fatal stroke in April of 1945. But that was, of course, scarcely the case: by the end of the year, she was engaged in myriad new causes, among them her role as delegate to the United Nations. And for subsequent generations of American women whose lives were immeasurably expanded by the inspiring example she set, the story was only beginning.

"It's better to light a candle than to curse the darkness."
—ER

WHAT PRICE LOVE

Few first ladies, to be sure, have ever been plagued by the problem of reporters who abjectly fawn over them. But newswoman Lorena Hickok, assigned in 1933 to cover Eleanor Roosevelt for the Associated Press, fell so hard for the president's wife that she lost all objectivity and finally had to quit her job. Previously enamored primarily of Pall Malls, cigars, and playing poker, two-hundred-pound "Hick" (as her colleagues called her) mooned over Eleanor's photo, marked her calendar with secret symbols to rate the quality of each and every one of their encounters, and even presented the first lady with an heirloom sapphire ring.

Though flattered by the attention, and truly fond of her scribbling suitor (the two women exchanged letters for the rest of their lives), Eleanor just couldn't commit. "I know you have a feeling for me which for one reason or another I may not return in kind," she wrote, "but I feel I love you just the same." To prove her friendship, the first lady gave hard-up Hick a gift perhaps even more precious than her passion—a free four-year stay in the White House from 1941 to 1945, one of the best-kept secrets in wartime Washington.

THE LIFE OF THE PARTY

The year was 1940, and many Americans were startled to learn that President Franklin D. Roosevelt, nearing the close of his second term in office, was seeking an unprecedented third. More mind-boggling still, however, was comedian Gracie Allen's declaration of her own intention to run for president as the candidate of the hitherto (and subsequently) obscure Surprise Party. "After all," she explained, "Mr. Roosevelt has been President for eight years, and I'm sure he wouldn't mind getting up and giving his seat to a lady." Though goofy Gracie didn't, of course, succeed in stealing the show from FDR, she did manage to garner several hundred write-in votes on election day, making the spoofy Surprise Party a truly unanticipated success.

A VEXING VISITOR

East was East, West was West, and...egalitarian Eleanor Roosevelt was simply aghast when Madame Chiang Kai-shek paid a twelve-day visit to Washington early in 1943. Her alleged enthusiasm for democratic principles notwithstanding, the Wellesley-educated wife of China's Nationalist leader traveled with an entourage of forty, clapped her hands to summon the servants, and insisted that White House maids launder her precious silk sheets (Madame didn't leave home without them) each and every day. Still, the flipped-out first lady tried to put her best foot forward, even procuring a rare century-old tea to please the Generalissimo's pride and joy. But the world's most ungracious guest refused to be impressed. "In my country," she informed her astounded hostess, "tea kept so long is used only for medicinal purposes."

A TRANSFORMATIONAL TRIANGLE
✷ ✷
HELL HATH NO FURY...

IF FRANKLIN ROOSEVELT SOMETIMES WISHED that he had a conventional stay-at-home wife, the thirty-second president of the United States had no one but himself to blame. During the first thirteen years of the Roosevelt marriage, it seems, Eleanor toed a traditional line, producing the requisite babies—six in all—and putting her man at the center of her life. And in 1914, she even hired twenty-two-year-old Lucy Mercer as an aide to help her help her husband—then the assistant secretary of the Navy—with his voluminous correspondence.

But as Franklin learned the hard way, it's never a good idea to keep love letters from other ladies lying around. In 1918, when Eleanor stumbled across literary evidence that FDR and Lucy were intimately involved, "the bottom dropped out of my world," and she bid adieu to acting the part of adoring wife. Although Franklin promised never to see his mistress again (largely, Eleanor suspected, because he feared the effects of scandal on his political career), Mrs. R insisted on separate bedrooms from that day on, pouring her passion into changing the world instead of preserving the rather shaky status quo.

Of course, Eleanor's constant sojourns to do good in one corner of the world or another might have made it even more tempting for FDR and Lucy (a real looker, according to one of the Roosevelt sons, with "a hint of fire in her warm eyes") to stray from the righteous path. But the inflammatory Mistress Mercer soon became the wife of a wealthy widower, and for more than twenty years, Franklin remained true to his word—and maybe even to his spouse. Not until the 1940s, during the final years of his administration, did Lucy secretly begin to visit the White House during the first lady's frequent absences, and passion bloom anew.

Despite his dalliance, however, the president sustained strong feelings for his wife. "I only wish she wasn't so darned busy," he told his son Elliot shortly before his death. "I could have her with me so much more if she didn't have so many other engagements." But the die had been cast decades earlier, and when FDR suffered his fatal stroke in April 1945, he was in the company of Lucy Mercer, and Eleanor was hard at work.

All things considered, the first lady received with equanimity the shocking news about Franklin's second fling, and when Lucy sent her a letter of condolence, she shot a sympathetic note right back. That noble gesture notwithstanding, however, Eleanor Roosevelt wasn't any more likely to sprout wings and fly than any other human being on earth. "I have the memory of an elephant," she confessed to her closest friends. "I can forgive, but I cannot forget."

> *"Work is almost the best way to pull oneself out of the depths."*
> —Eleanor Roosevelt

TO THE VICTOR GO THE SPOILS

As the wife of the well-known New York governor/two-time GOP presidential candidate, Frances Dewey had heard more than her share of ephemeral campaign promises. So when husband Thomas bragged in November 1948 that she'd soon be sleeping with the president of the United States, Frances fully intended to hold him to his word. "Am I going to Washington or is Harry coming here?" she inquired brightly when she learned that her self-assured spouse hadn't beaten the pants off President Truman after all.

MARGUERITE LEHAND

✭ ✭

ANOTHER OF FRANKLIN'S FEMMES

"IT IS DISGRACEFUL," an irate White House visitor once wrote to Eleanor Roosevelt. Because the first lady was seldom found at home, she maintained, the president's residence had slipped into a state of neglect so severe that "I soiled my white gloves yesterday morning on the stair-railing." Certainly, one imagines, housekeeping standards may have sagged somewhat between 1933 and 1945, given the national and global Sturm and Drang the Roosevelts faced during those years. Yet thanks to some rather avant-garde domestic arrangements at 1600 Pennsylvania Avenue, the president himself never suffered from want of a feminine touch. While Eleanor gallivanted hither and yon promoting her humanitarian causes, it seems, the stately Marguerite "Missy" LeHand, who occupied a third-floor apartment in the mansion, gladly filled in as Franklin's wife.

Technically speaking, Missy (thirty-seven when she accompanied the Roosevelts to the White House in 1933) drew her salary as FDR's personal secretary, rather than as his spouse. But family intimates all agreed that her behavior suggested otherwise. "As close to being a wife," according to one insider, "as [Franklin] ever had," the devoted Ms. LeHand paid the president's personal bills, planned his menus, took an encouraging interest in his stamp collection, and sometimes interrupted state meetings to remind him to take his cough syrup or put on a warmer sweater. Elegant in chandelier earrings and a glamorous nightgown (which she favored, for whatever reason, over more conventional evening wear), she served as hostess while Mrs. R was away, and, as the first lady could tolerate neither spirits nor small talk, did the honors at the evening cocktail hour even when she was not. And when a Roosevelt offspring wanted his allowance, Missy (and not his mom) was the benefactress to whom he turned.

But Franklin's acting Mrs. did more than preside, as one acquaintance put it, "with a queenly dignity as a substitute for the apparently unmentionable First Lady of the Land." No correspondence left the president's desk if Missy deemed its tone too sarcastic, and FDR once scrapped a proposed speech on finance that she deemed unbearably boring—an opinion she expressed by ostentatiously leaving the room. "She was one of the few people who could say 'No' to the President and say it in a way he could take," recalled one White House aide.

As to the truly crucial question of whether Missy said aye or nay to bedding the boss, however, not even FDR's closest family members would later agree. (Not likely, some claimed, due to his paralysis, though according to his doctor, no medical obstacle stood in the way of intimacy.) But after Missy suffered an incapacitating stroke at the age of forty-five, the lady in the grimy white gloves would have been either pleased or perplexed to know, the *real* Mrs. Roosevelt did rise to the occasion and act, however fleetingly, exactly like a wife. Under the sad circumstances, the first lady reminded Franklin, whose mind was apparently on other matters, a visit to his surrogate spouse would only be fitting and proper.

> *"He might have been happier with a wife who was completely uncritical. That I was never able to be, and he had to find it in other people."*
> —Eleanor Roosevelt

BLESSED BY BIRTH

★ ★

MAMA'S BOYS

THOUGH OLD MAIDS WERE DISTINCTLY OUT of fashion in the mid-1800s, twentyish Louisa Torrey was perfectly content to teach school, travel, and revel in her single—if always slightly impecunious— state. Marriage, she shuddered, "would be a disagreeable expedient...I had rather economize." And even after she bowed to the inevitable and settled down in 1853 with spouse Alphonso Taft and (eventually) six children, level-headed Louisa ran her household more like a business than a birthing center. "When the woman's field widens, Mother, you must become president of a Railroad Company," son William Howard once fawned in a loving letter home. Of course, if the "woman's field" had been just a tad less constricted in Louisa's heyday, young Will—the twenty-seventh president of the United States—might well have never been born. Or, perhaps, Louisa would have held the paramount position in lieu of her son.

★ ★ ★

CATAPULTED TO THE PRESIDENCY BY FDR'S death in April 1945, former V.P. Harry S. Truman was too tied up at the office to make it home for Mother's Day that May. Rather than miss out on her holiday, however, ninety-two-year-old Mother Truman simply transported herself from Missouri to Washington (via, interestingly enough, the presidential aircraft known as "The Sacred Cow"). Suffice it to say that upon Mrs. T's much-heralded arrival, it immediately became apparent that "Give 'Em Hell" Harry came honestly by that tinderbox temperament. "Oh, fiddlesticks!" blustered the president's annoyed parent as she emerged from the plane and reporters started snapping her photo left and right. "If I'd have known there was going to be all this fuss, I wouldn't have come."

★ ★ ★

NEARLY AS FAMOUS—AND NEARLY AS FALSE—as the old saw about George and the cherry tree is Abraham Lincoln's oft-quoted tribute to his dear mama, who died in 1818 at the age of thirty-four: "All that I am or hope ever to be I get from my mother." Not that Honest Abe, one understands, was constitutionally capable of telling a fib. But historians who handed down the comment out of context were certainly guilty of a small sin of omission. Crucial to the significance of the statement, it seems, is the intriguing fact that the president attributed Mama Lincoln's superior mental powers to her illegitimate birth. "Did you never notice that bastards are generally smarter, shrewder, and more intellectual than others?" he remarked—in the same breath, it happens, as he issued that Hallmark platitude about all the good stuff he got from Mom.

YES, DEAR, AND I SUPPOSE
THE DOG ATE YOUR HOMEWORK

Behind every great man, it seems, is a woman...who is very, very surprised. To wit, Woodrow Wilson's elderly aunt, who was startled to hear in 1912 that her nephew had just become president of...something or the other. "Of the United States," clarified Wilson, who had, after all, also served a term as president of Princeton University. Not having been born yesterday, however, Wilson's wily old auntie wasn't anybody's fool. "Don't be silly!" she scolded, putting the fifty-six-year-old president-elect squarely in his (junior-sized) place.

BESS TRUMAN

✶ ✶

HARRY'S SILENT PARTNER

NO, BESS TRUMAN WASN'T ANY ELEANOR ROOSEVELT—nor did she aspire to be. "I couldn't possibly be anything like her," bristled privacy-loving Bess who, as fate would have it, was forced to take up White House residence in 1945, hard on the heels of the most noteworthy first lady in history. "I wasn't going down in any coal mines."

When members of the press solicited interviews with Eleanor's reluctant successor, temperamental Mrs. Truman clammed right up and wouldn't utter a peep. "It's none of their d— business," she snapped in response to reporters' inquiries about what she planned to wear on any particular occasion. Despite the precedent set by her recent predecessors, Bess simply refused to promote a cause. Elizabeth Monroe, one of the most adamantly reclusive first ladies ever (and also one of the most unpopular), she stoutly maintained, served as her personal model. "I am not the one elected," she insisted. "I have nothing to say to the public."

In years to come, First Daughter Margaret would speculate that Mom's passion for privacy stemmed from the hushed-up suicide of her father in 1903— a big stigma to live down in the old-fashioned town of Independence, Missouri. (Lucky for the taciturn first lady, reporters bent on sussing out the color of her ball gowns never stumbled across the secret that would certainly have made a juicier story.) But behind closed doors, by all accounts, Bess's verbal reticence miraculously vanished.

Certainly husband Harry, celebrated for his crackling curses, got an earful from his wife every time he mouthed off in public. "The madam thinks I shouldn't have any more press conferences," he confessed after reports circulated that he'd called one Arkansas senator "an overeducated s.o.b." And when one delicate dowager objected to Harry's use of the term "manure," Bess retorted that she'd struggled for years to get her husband to use that particular word instead of the considerably less elegant vernacular.

Unbeknownst to voters, however, the first lady's influence over the president extended far beyond cleaning up his vocabulary. According to Truman family intimates, in fact, HST's better half passed most of her White House evenings locked away with her husband in his study, offering her analysis and advice regarding everything from minor speeches to the Marshall Plan, and allegedly even the controversial decision to drop the atomic bomb on Hiroshima in August 1945. Nor, whatever the electorate might make of it, did it strike Harry as strange (any more than it would so strike Hillary Clinton's husband nearly thirty years later) to solicit the opinion of the Mrs. "She looks at things objectively and I can't always," he explained. And long after stepping down from the presidency in 1953, Harry publicly praised his wife as his "chief advisor" and "full partner in all transactions—politically and otherwise."

All the spousal respect in the world, however, never did persuade Bess (who pointedly referred to the White House as "The Great White Jail") to relish her prominent role. And when one reporter dared to inquire, late in 1948, how she liked being first lady, Bess's response was as delightfully un-Eleanoresque as ever. "Oh, so-so," responded the president's reluctant right-hand woman.

"You don't need to know me. I'm only the president's wife and the mother of his daughter."
—BT

MARGARET TRUMAN

✷ ✷

THOSE OLD UNEMPLOYMENT BLUES

WHEN TWENTY-ONE-YEAR-OLD MARGARET TRUMAN took up White House residence with Mom and Pop in 1945, the aspiring concert soprano/college coed thought she had it made. But during the next seven years, life in the limelight didn't prove quite as gratifying as the president's daughter had hoped. For one thing, Mrs. Truman was mightily determined that Margaret, her one-and-only child, not develop a swollen head. Big Bess gave her the evil eye when she caught her "preening" in public, took her to task for dating a playboy when she read about it in the paper, and wouldn't even allow Margaret little luxuries like a coveted mink scarf unless she could pay for them herself.

But Mama needn't have worried—Margaret never had a chance to be spoiled by success. Though her prominent parentage certainly helped her land some impressive singing gigs (in 1947, she made her concert debut with Eugene Normandy and the Hollywood Bowl Symphony), it also caused reviewers to deconstruct her performances with singular zest. Even members of the White House staff, it seemed, blossomed overnight into critics when it came to Margaret's musical talent. "We had to be as careful of the young star as though she were a fragile rose," grumbled a Truman-era maid. "No one dared raise dust anywhere near her sensitive nose." Also, she recalled, the would-be concert artist's proboscis was problematic in more ways than one: behind her back, employees speculated that Margaret didn't stand a chance in show biz unless she fixed that prominent feature.

In December 1950, however, *Washington Post* critic Paul Hume effectively scotched Ms. Truman's budding career without the slightest reference to rhinoplasty, jeering that not only was the president's daughter "flat a good deal of the time," but she could not "sing with anything approaching professional finish." Shortly thereafter, a major parental boo-boo made Margaret's mortification complete. Enraged by Hume's derogatory review, the famously hot-headed president fired off a poison pen letter to the critic, seething that "I never met you, but if I do you'll need a new nose and a supporter below."

Not for nothing, however, was the humiliated ex-singer the offspring of "Give 'Em Hell" Harry. Shrugging off the very public failure of her first career, she went on to enjoy a far more successful second vocation as the author of several volumes on presidential history, as well as numerous popular murder mysteries set in the nation's capital. Therapeutic as the opportunity (indeed, the professional obligation) to indulge freely in homicidal fantasy may have proven, however, Margaret apparently never did figure out how to extinguish a lingering sense of regret. "Because my father was the President," she wrote in 1981, decades after abandoning her musical ambitions, "I had to be not better than average but better than the best."

> *"Of course we were very proud of her—really more because she had nerve enough to do it than of her performance."*
> —Bess Truman

HENRIETTA NESBITT AND ZEPHYR WRIGHT

✶ ✶

THE COLDEST CUTS OF ALL

L EFT TO HER OWN DEVICES by domestically indifferent Eleanor, presidential housekeeper Henrietta Nesbitt once fed FDR and his Cabinet mutton and boiled carrots for a supposedly classy dinner. But that was a gala feast compared to the usual White House fare in the thirties and forties. Nasty Nesbitt doled out broccoli by the boxcar load, served up sweetbreads six times a week when the president complained of too much chicken, and was, judging by the record, completely unaware that anything other than oatmeal might be consumed at the morning meal.

But apparently such culinary insults weren't intended as a personal slur on the Roosevelts—the dour White House domestic dished out the same chilly treatment to former V.P. Harry Truman and his family when they suddenly entered her sphere of influence after FDR's death in 1945. As soon as the newly inaugurated prez made his distaste for brussels sprouts known, those vile veggies turned up on his plate three nights in a row. And when wife Bess requested a stick of butter to take to a potluck, Nesbitt turned the first lady down cold—the White House, she huffed, might run short on ration stamps, and couldn't spare so much as a smidgen of lard. Several weeks into the new administration, the Trumans finally rebelled against the tyrannical Nesbitt regime, and another institution of the Roosevelt era went marching out the door.

Some twenty years later, however, another White House prima donna came up with a far superior method of biting the hand she fed—she went straight to the *Washington Post* with her culinary woes. According to Zephyr Wright, the cook charged with the Texas-sized task of keeping Lyndon Johnson's larder stocked, LBJ was one tough customer to please. For one thing, she tattled, the boss thought nothing of bringing two dozen cronies home for lunch—on fifteen minutes' notice. On other occasions, he didn't manage to make the dinner table until two hours after the scheduled time for the meal, then blew a fuse when his popovers were no longer in their prime. And despite the fact that Wright made a point of serving LBJ the low-cal meals recommended by his M.D., the president put on nearly thirty pounds during his term in office. After he dutifully downed a diet special, it seems, he'd polish off a regular dinner as well.

Unlike her predecessor Henrietta Nesbitt, however, LBJ's chatty cook didn't allow personal peeves to completely destroy her career. On the bright side, after all, learning to cope with the stress of her station made Wright—who ballooned, she told the *Post*, from 130 to 210 pounds during her five years in the White House—much, much more of a woman.

> *"Housekeeping ain't no joke."*
> —Louisa May Alcott in *Little Women*

ANOTHER MUSICAL MARGARET

Though First Daughter Margaret Wilson debuted as a singer with the Chicago Symphony Orchestra in 1915, White House guests apparently tolerated her quavers and trills with less than total enthusiasm. Visitors, gossiped one staffer, did not consider performances by Woodrow Wilson's thirtyish daughter "a treat; it was simply the price of being invited." After a second short-lived career as a copywriter and a third speculating in stocks, the scorned soprano finally fled to a religious community in India, where she lived the rest of her life in virtual isolation.

IV

AFFAIRS OF STATE IN THE
FIFTIES AND SIXTIES

KAY SUMMERSBY

* *

SHE DROVE HIM TO IT

KAY SUMMERSBY LIKED IKE—a lot. For three never-to-be-forgotten years, the beautiful Irish-born Londoner and the five-star American general who was soon to be president carried on a passionate secret affair, while World War II raged across Europe—and Mamie waited at home.

"More than half my life I have felt like the girl in the hair-coloring advertisement," Summersby wrote at the end of her life, "the one that asks the question, 'Does she...or doesn't she?'" Yes, it seems, she did...and spilled every last romantic detail (as well as less ethereal tidbits about Winston Churchill's table manners, the consequences of too much English cabbage, and her lover's numerous illnesses) in *Past Forgetting*, her poignant memoir of wartime love and betrayal.

Frankly, Summersby—a thirtyish, soon-to-be-divorced former fashion model—wasn't thrilled when Britain's Motor Transport Corps ("the volunteer corps that the debutantes...flocked to") assigned her to chauffeur the distinctly unglamorous fifty-two-year-old general around town during his 1942 mission in London. But when Summersby joined Eisenhower's personal staff in Algiers in the autumn of 1943, the relationship blossomed—right, in the finest Hollywood tradition, in the middle of a spat. "You are a goddamned stubborn Irish mule," the general remarked romantically. "Goddamnit, can't you tell I'm crazy about you?" Suddenly, Summersby recalled, they were in each other's arms; his "hungry, strong, demanding" kisses, she sighed, "absolutely unraveled me."

Naturally, there were obstacles to the course of true love. Many months (and many unraveling kisses) later, Eisenhower revealed, or so Summersby claimed, that his sexless marriage to Mamie had left him unable to be "the lover you should have." Also, she noted dryly, the Supreme Commander of the Allied

Forces in Europe "had much more than me, Kay Summersby, on his mind." Still, when Eisenhower returned to the United States in November 1945, it was with the understanding that Summersby would shortly join him in the Pentagon as a member of his personal staff—and more.

But the reunion never took place, and Summersby never made it to the White House in any capacity. Eisenhower, of course, went on to renew his relationship with Mamie and become the thirty-fourth president of the United States, and his jilted mistress, who never received any explanation for the estrangement, fell in love with and married another man. Not until 1976 would Summersby stumble across the reason for the rift in Merle Miller's oral biography of Harry Truman, which revealed that General George Marshall, U.S. Army Chief of Staff, had informed Eisenhower that he could kiss his military career good-bye if he dumped Mamie for his dashing female driver.

By that late date, however, Summersby wasn't devastated (or even surprised) to learn that her now-deceased lover's ardor had been sacrificed on the altar of his ambition. ("Goddamnit, don't cry," she imagined him barking impatiently.) Besides, as they say in the movies, she'd still always have...Algiers.

"I believe that truth makes for better history than evasions."
—KS

MAMIE EISENHOWER

✦ ✦

RELAXED IN HER ROLE

SOME INDEPENDENT FIRST LADIES thought of the White House as a high-security prison on the Potomac. Others, more enthralled with their fifteen minutes (or four years) of fame, considered it a lovely bully pulpit. But only Mamie Eisenhower—the fluffy, pink-clad consort of manly General Ike—thought that 1600 Pennsylvania Avenue was the address of her own personal spa.

"Every woman over fifty should stay in bed until noon," declared Mamie, an aggressively youthful fifty-seven when Ike took office in 1953, and she wouldn't be pried from between her rose-colored sheets a moment sooner. Not that every moment in Mamie's private boudoir was devoted to snoozing: propped comfortably against her pillows, she perused her correspondence, dispensed orders to White House staff, and directed her avid attention to *As the World Turns*. Soap operas, sighed the luxuriously recumbent first lady (who officially pooh-poohed rumors of her husband's adulterous affair), were so "true to life." Meanwhile, across the hall, Mamie's doting mama reposed in similar splendor, preferring to chat by phone with "Sleeping Beauty" (as staff soon dubbed her daughter) rather than disrupt her own sacrosanct beauty rest.

Needless to say, the president's wife wasn't expected to lift a freshly mani-cured finger around the White House—save, perhaps, to draw it languidly across a window ledge when she suspected the staff wasn't performing up to snuff. But unlike most other first ladies, who maintained at least a nodding acquaintance with the kitchen (even overextended Eleanor whipped up those legendary Sunday scrambled eggs herself), Mamie pleaded ignorance when it came to producing anything more substantial than her famous fudge. Besides, she explained ingenuously, "Ike cooks anything better than anybody, that's why I hate to work hard over a meal."

Meals, however, were not the only thing that Mamie hated "to work hard over." Charming visitors or delighting her fans by popping up unexpectedly in the midst of a parade was one thing—Mamie even posed on an elevated platform while receiving guests to make sure that America got a good look (and also to save her from shaking too many hands). But the concept of curtailing her afternoon bridge parties in order to take on a pet project appalled the pampered first lady. Even an invitation to write a daily newspaper column along the lines of

A real lounge lizard

Eleanor Roosevelt's "My Day" was rejected out of hand—"It sounds like a terrible chore." And when the *Washington Post* slammed the first lady's tacit policy of "inactivism," Mamie didn't fret for long—after all, Ike pointed out, it was easy enough simply to stop reading the paper.

Looking back on her days as the cosseted first lady of the fabulous fifties, Mamie freely admitted that "I loved being in the White House." But then again, as the best-rested president's wife in history gloated to Rosalynn Carter in 1977, "I was never expected to do all the things you have to do."

"I never knew what a woman would want to be liberated from."
—ME

JACQUELINE KENNEDY

✮ ✮

AN ENTHRALLING ENIGMA

ELEGANT JACQUELINE KENNEDY DRIFTED into the White House in 1961 murmuring of fox hunts and antique furniture, utterly indifferent to what the masses might make of her demeanor. "The American people just aren't ready for someone like you," sighed husband Jack. "I guess we'll just have to run you through subliminally in one of those quick flash TV spots so no one will notice." Yet like a pretty child, or a movie star, the mercurial Mrs. Kennedy was much admired, apparently simply because she was, not because she went out of her way to make herself warm or winning.

To the aristocratic Queen of Camelot, the title "First Lady" held little mystique. "It sounds like a saddle horse," she complained, and forbade White House staff to use the term. And often, it seemed, Jackie wanted to be a first lady no more than she wanted to be called one. She refused to attend Congressional Wives' prayer breakfasts, nor could she be bothered with a luncheon the Wives held in her honor. (While Jackie took in a performance of the London Royal Ballet, the president took her place at the banquet table.) And though she won praise for restoring (and not, she insisted, "redecorating") the White House to the nineteenth-century French Empire style, the task also provided an excuse to ignore less compelling duties. "Why should I traipse around to hospitals playing Lady Bountiful when I have so much to do here to make this house livable?" she shrugged.

Jackie's aesthetic discretion wasn't exercised solely on interior decorating, of course. Her sartorial goal, she informed designer Oleg Cassini, was to dress as though "Jack were President of France"—and "no fat little women hopping around in the same gown," please. Nonetheless, everyone from socialites to shopgirls copied the first lady's couture as though it were Holy Writ. After she was photographed with a slight (and accidental) dent in that well-known pillbox hat, bashed-in chapeaus were suddenly all the rage. And when she sported a $3,000 leopard skin coat on the cover of *Life,* reported the designer Halston, the price of similar furs jumped to $40,000, and leopards would up on the endangered species list.

Glamorous Mrs. K

Preoccupied with her own artsy concerns, Jackie took little interest in the professional life of the president. An ex-Republican who, until she met JFK, had never even bothered to vote, she once observed to friends that Acapulco might make a nice site for the next Democratic Convention (and was puzzled by the subsequent laughter). Yet after an assassin's bullet tragically terminated Jack Kennedy's life in November 1963, many thought his widow should run for the Senate, or even seek the nomination for vice president. According to a 1964 Gallup poll, Americans admired no woman in the world more than Jackie. And although her halo slipped slightly after her marriage to Aristotle Onassis, few who lived through the golden days of Camelot (and few who didn't, as well) would ever cease to be fascinated by the first lady who flaunted her champagne tastes. Jackie, as one friend put it, wasn't "as American as apple pie"; she was "as American as caviar."

> *"People have told me ninety-nine things that I had to do as First Lady, and I haven't done one of them."*
> —JK

THE POLITICS OF PASSION

★ ★

JKF'S FRISKIEST PLAYMATES

WAS POWER THE SECRET APHRODISIAC of President John F. Kennedy? Was it the revolutionary new birth control pill, available in the U.S. just a few months after his 1961 inauguration? Or simply the handsome New Englander's own personal charm? Though some of the following accounts should be taken with a grain of salt, no other administration has ever left behind such a lurid legacy of bedtime stories...

THE GREAT PHILANDERER supposedly celebrated his presidential nomination in 1960 by skinny-dipping with actress Angie Dickinson, and his inauguration in a similarly unfettered fashion (though this time without the pool). And supposedly, too, the leggy TV star found her romantic rendezvous with the nation's leader "the most remarkable sixty seconds of my life."

★　★　★

"THIS COUNTRY KNOWS MORE about Jayne [Mansfield]'s statistics than about the Second Commandment," the Reverend Billy Graham once complained. One bit of data of which few were apprised, however, was that the curvaceous movie star's trysts with President Kennedy numbered three. (The Second Commandment, by the way, isn't the one about adultery.)

★　★　★

NEW YORK CALL GIRL Leslie Devereux was taken aback when JFK proposed a roll in Abraham Lincoln's enormous rosewood bed—to her, the site seemed "sacrilegious." But the president laid on a persuasive line: according to White House legend, he claimed, any wish made on the Lincoln bed would magically come true. And, according to Devereux, his certainly did.

★ ★ ★

IN MAY 1962, SUPER-SEX-SYMBOL Marilyn Monroe wriggled into a $12,000 "skin and beads" gown and treated President Kennedy and a mesmerized Madison Garden crowd to the breathiest version of "Happy Birthday" the world has ever heard. Actually, of course, JFK's most famous mistress could have warbled in his ear any old time, since she had her own private line to the White House.

★ ★ ★

A DIVORCÉE EIGHT TIMES OVER, actress Zsa Zsa Gabor was scarcely in a position to covet another woman's one-and-only. Besides, her fling with Jack Kennedy was quite kaput in 1953, when her seatmate on a transatlantic flight turned out to be Jacqueline Bouvier, JFK's future bride. Nonetheless, the haughty Hungarian couldn't find a kind word for her former lover's fiancée. "She had kinky hair and bad skin," Gabor later revealed. "She wasn't the most glamorous woman."

★ ★ ★

MARY PINCHOT MEYER, whom JFK managed to sneak into the White House more than thirty times, had high hopes for her secret lover. A pal of LSD guru Timothy Leary, the avant-garde artist planned to turn all world leaders on to pot and acid, thereby making them more mellow. During the course of the two-year relationship, Meyer (the sister-in-law of *Washington Post* publisher Ben Bradlee) certainly did her bit for peace: not only did Kennedy light up with mistress Mary, but he allegedly tripped out on one occasion as well. Ironically, JFK's persuasive antiviolence advocate was murdered just ten months after the November 1963 tragedy in Dallas, and the crime remains unsolved to this day. A diary found after Meyer's death, however, left few details of her love life to the imagination.

★   ★   ★

SWINGING WHITE HOUSE SECRETARIES Priscilla "Fiddle" Weir and Jill "Faddle" Cowan shared an apartment. And even Jackie was in on the scuttlebutt that the daring duo sometimes also shared her man. "This is one of the young ladies who is supposed to be sleeping with my husband," the first lady offhandedly informed a visiting French journalist when she introduced him to Fiddle...or, for whatever difference it might make, to Faddle.

★   ★   ★

IN 1958, THEN-SENATOR JOHN KENNEDY found his receptionist, Pamela Turnure, far too alluring to resist. But Turnure's old-fashioned landlords, Flo and Leonard Kater, were determined to stop the legislator's extramarital shenanigans with their tenant. When the couple bombarded the press with sexy photos of the senator, however, every paper except the *Washington Star* ignored the story. By the time her bed partner became president, Turnure had found herself a happier home, as well as a job as (of all things) Jackie Kennedy's press secretary, but the Katers picketed the White House on Inauguration Day anyway, flaunting a sign that read "DO YOU WANT AN ADULTERER IN THE WHITE HOUSE?" At the time, of course, everyone thought they were absolute kooks.

REVOLT OF THE JUMBO MAMAS

It was no secret during the Johnson administration that LBJ suffered from a weakness for women—but only the fashionably slender kind. "I can't stand an ugly woman around or a fat one who looks like a cow that's gonna step on her own udder," he once confided to an aide.

Women who didn't want to tangle with the aesthetically aware Texan dieted and dyed like mad: Lady Bird's press secretary munched on Metrecal cookies to please him, while the first lady herself tried to beautify all of America. But LBJ's final months in office weren't pleasant ones in terms of pulchritude: after he announced that he wouldn't seek reelection in 1968, loyal staffers stopped postponing their reproductive plans, and bovine bellies started popping up all over the White House.

JUDITH CAMPBELL EXNER

✶ ✶

THE MATA HARI OF CAMELOT

I PREFERRED THE COMPANY OF MEN to that of women," Los Angeles socialite Judith Campbell Exner once admitted. Evidently so. In her heyday as the "In" date of the 1960s, Exner (a dark-haired beauty who resembled Elizabeth Taylor) engaged in overlapping liaisons with an eclectic cadre of American elites—among them entertainer Frank Sinatra, President John F. Kennedy, and Chicago mob boss Sam Giancana. But in 1975, the playgirl whose bedmates included both a mafioso and the man in the White House suddenly found herself in demand with a very different sort of suitor: the U.S. Senate committee investigating CIA/Mafia collaboration in a fifteen-year-old plot to assassinate Fidel Castro.

Despite the heady company she once kept, insisted Exner (first to the Senate committee, and again in her 1977 autobiography), plain old-fashioned romance was all she ever had on her mind. When Kennedy inquired during their initial rendezvous whether she "was a Democrat or a Republican," his twenty-six-year-old date "honestly confessed that I didn't know." (Apparently in Exner's book, a political party was only a festive occasion involving Jack Daniels, a VIP, and an interlude in the boudoir.) And though she and Kennedy enjoyed at least twenty White House trysts during his first two years in office, only intimate details about the president's fondness for catsup, sloppy clothing, and passive sex—and not, for example, his stance on Communist Cuba—really stuck in Exner's mind. ("I loved the way he pronounced 'hustings,'" she recalled.)

Equally eyebrow-raising was Exner's claim that she never inquired how Giancana, the showy Chicago escort who, under the pseudonym of "Sam Flood," showered her with jewelry and roses in five-dozen bunches, actually earned his dough. Although she often flew directly from a White House assignation to a rendezvous with her other big-name beau, Exner swore that she never discussed one man with the other.

Mortality, however, has a way of putting things in a different perspective. "I don't think I should have to die with the secret of what I did for Jack Kennedy, or what he did with the power of his Presidency," fifty-four-year-old Exner observed in 1988. Then suffering from terminal cancer, she proceeded to tell Kitty Kelley of *People* magazine precisely what the Senate committee may have suspected all along: the specialized services she provided to JFK included couriering top-secret communiqués between the president and the mob chief. And although Exner claimed never to have examined the envelopes she carried, she suspected, in hindsight, that she had inadvertently helped her lover "orchestrate the attempted assassination of Fidel Castro with the Mafia."

As to whether JFK's glamorous paramour regretted her shocking undercover role in the Kennedy administration, however, the record was never entirely clear. "My interest in Jack, my need to be with him, was stronger than my conscience," admitted Exner, sounding like any other sadder, wiser, but not necessarily repentant adulterer in the world.

"To be perfectly honest about it, I think I was caught up a little with the intrigue of it."
—JE

PARTY POOPERS

* *

GALS WHO GAVE JACK THE BOOT

NO, THE THIRTY-FIFTH PRESIDENT of the United States didn't do the deed with every comely Democrat in the country. History reveals that at least two zany trendbuckers declined to hop aboard JFK's bedroom bandwagon. And just like every ordinary Joe, even the Casanova of the Oval Office once had his heart shattered by a woman he truly loved...

THE KENNEDY BRAND OF FRIENDLINESS didn't do a thing for actress Shirley MacLaine, who first encountered the prez in the limo of mutual pal Frank Sinatra in 1961. Startled to get a hands-on greeting instead of a simple hello, MacLaine bolted from the slow-moving vehicle and skinned her knee in the process. But evidently she didn't hold a grudge regarding the grope. "I would rather have a President who does it to a woman than a President who does it to his country," she later concluded.

* * *

JOINING SHIRLEY MACLAINE in the exclusive "I Never Slept with JFK" club was fellow actress Marlene Dietrich. A seasoned soul of sixty when Kennedy took office in 1961, Dietrich was a former lover of the president's father. But a sixteen-year age gap didn't prevent Jack from making amorous advances toward Dad's old flame when he invited her to the White House—or her from forcefully rebuffing them. As Dietrich once shrugged: "They always want to put their things in. That's all they want."

⋆   ⋆   ⋆

IN 1942, TWENTY-FIVE-YEAR-OLD naval ensign John F. Kennedy went gaga for Danish journalist Inga Arvad, a divorcée four years his senior. The CIA, however, wasn't thrilled when it discovered that Jack's honey had interviewed Adolf Hitler during the 1936 Olympics, subsequently describing the Nazi dictator as "very kind, very charming." A wiretap of Arvad's Washington apartment revealed nothing more incriminating about the Kennedy/Arvad alliance than JFK's tendency to call his girlfriend "Inga Binga" in moments of passion. But the affair cracked under the strain of constant government surveillance, and the Dane soon ditched her Navy guy and got herself hitched to cowboy film star Tim McCoy instead.

THE SWEETIE WITH A SCREW LOOSE

Never one to discourage female access to the presidential person, JFK commanded his Secret Service to admit certain comely constituents without extensive screening. On one occasion, he even insisted that an unknown eighteen-year-old Irishwoman be sent directly to the Oval Office to shake his hand. Any potential flesh-pressing had to be scrapped, however, when agents discovered that the visitor was a stranger in more ways than one, recently released from a psychiatric institution in Dublin, and toting a fourteen-inch butcher knife in her (presumably rather humongous) handbag.

JANET TRAVELL

✱ ✱

JFK'S ROCKIN' DOC

U NLIKE THE BEVY OF STARLETS and seductresses that surrounded JFK, Dr. Janet Travell took a strictly professional interest in the presidential bod. The first woman to serve as personal physician to a U.S. president (though Grover Cleveland sought the services of a Dr. Anna Easton, her own ill health prevented her from accepting), Travell first treated the fledgling Massachusetts senator for crippling back pain following spinal surgery in 1955. "She's the reason I'm alive today," Kennedy commented when, six years later, he asked the Cornell University Medical College alum to follow him to the White House.

Though skeptics found Travell's acupuncture-like methods of controlling muscle spasms suspiciously unorthodox (perhaps not coincidentally, she spent a large part of her girlhood conducting electrical experiments on frogs), her exclusive appointment disappointed other patients who also relied on the healing touch of her "large, gnarled" (or so one magazine writer had it) hand. "I'm just going to have to work out a back-door arrangement with Jack," sighed Kennedy's long-term political foe Barry Goldwater, who often consulted the controversial medic for chronic conditions of the back and arm.

A remarkably hip fifty-nine-year-old grandmother (not to mention a registered Republican) amidst the swinging court of Camelot, Travell didn't miss a beat when her notoriously libidinous boss balked at an injection that would, she advised, temporarily "eliminate all sensation below the waist." As part of the president's long-term treatment, the down-to-earth doc also prescribed a daily plunge in the pool—a suggestion Kennedy not only followed faithfully, but encouraged others (particularly, it seems, ladies who looked nice in the nude) to adopt as well. If JFK felt no pain during the legendary daiquiri-and-skinny-dipping parties that sometimes erupted on Jackie-less days at 1600 Pennsylvania Avenue, Travell was the woman to thank, or blame.

Less sexy than aquatics *au naturel* (though certainly more so than JFK's out-of-water orthopedic shoes) was Travell's most peculiar prescription for her glamorous patient: the gentle muscle stimulus provided by the use of a nice old-fashioned rocking chair. Well, seemingly less sexy: when word got out that far-from-geriatric Jack had installed a $24.95 rocker in his White House office, groupies across the country caught rocker fever, and demand for the Kennedy model suddenly shot sky-high. Not quite as high, however, as the $453,500 that Travell's much-touted chair would eventually fetch at the 1996 auction of Jacqueline Kennedy Onassis' estate—a sum that even a layperson might definitively describe as healthy.

"The mind can absorb no more than the seat can endure."
—JT

LETITIA BALDRIGE

✶ ✶

STAFF GAFFES

THOUGH ETIQUETTE EXPERT LETITIA BALDRIGE wrote the book on Grade-A deportment (not to mention updating two of Amy Vanderbilt's how-to-behave tomes), her own performance as Jacqueline Kennedy's social secretary was far from flawless. Speaking a little too off-the-cuff at her premiere press conference in November 1960, Baldrige described the charismatic Jackie, an old Vassar friend, as "a woman who has everything, including the next President of the United States." (Unlike Baldrige's audience, the boss was not amused.)

Next, her passing reference to members of ladies' clubs who would soon be clamoring for the first lady's attention as "those great vast hordes of females" set the sharp little teeth of upper-crust women from San Francisco to Schenectady on edge. ("I mean those large groups of very interesting ladies," Baldrige self-edited, somewhat belatedly.) For some reason, her announcement that the Kennedy White House would serve as "a showcase for great American artists" set off a panic that historic treasures were about to be dumped in lieu of bizarre modern art. And, lest Baldrige survive her grueling public debut minus any permanent psychic scars, at least one subsequent report misidentified her chic ocelot hat, carefully chosen for the occasion, as "gaudy leopardskin."

Soon relieved of her obligation to address the press, Baldrige was next assigned to concentrate her energies on organizing the swank, culturally significant extravaganzas for which the Kennedys would become so well known. Her first endeavor along these lines, however, landed the president himself in hot water. Setting up a hard liquor bar at a White House reception (on a Sunday evening, at that), numerous Bible Belt congressmen hastened to inform their host, wasn't quite the done thing. "How can one give a cocktail party without cocktails?" wondered Baldrige (who had, as it happened, spent several years acquiring worldly sophistication in Paris) after a hopping mad JFK called her on the carpet.

But although Baldrige departed rather prematurely from her post in 1963, complaining of exhaustion and a measly government salary that didn't begin to cover the ball gowns and jewels that she needed to adequately perform her job, the burned-out social secretary took away more than a modicum of new-found savoir faire. "One must toss off today's crisis with a shrug," she observed. Not, one understands, as a matter of protocol, but one of practicality: "Tomorrow's," explained Baldrige, "will be far worse."

> *"You will make lots of mistakes, and you must learn*
> *only not to suffer because of them."*
> —Edith Helm, social secretary to
> Edith Wilson and Eleanor Roosevelt

UNDERCOVER IN THE WHITE HOUSE

✯ ✯

HALF-SLIPS AND FULL-FLEDGED FAUX PAS

O WEAR OR TO BARE? That was Mamie Eisenhower's perplexing dilemma during the 1953 state visit of Queen Frederika of Greece. An ungloved hand, the all-American first lady finally decided, was ever so much more friendly to shake (and the hell with royal protocol), so she greeted the Greek with a pale pink palm. Not every garment abandoned in the White House, however, appears to have been doffed pursuant to such serious contemplation as Mamie's glove...

DELICATE INTERNATIONAL RELATIONS TEETERED in the balance when a foreign diplomat's wife suddenly lost her drawers while standing in line to be received by FDR. The day (not to mention the unmentionable) was saved by White House doorman John Mays, who unobtrusively plucked the offending apparel from the floor, folded it over his arm like a tea towel, and suavely bore it out of sight.

✯ ✯ ✯

DURING AN ESPECIALLY LIVELY LBJ DO, noted *New York Daily News* columnist Judith Axler, one glamorous guest "felt her horsehair petticoat beginning to slip...so she quickly kicked it under the nine-foot-long gilded grand piano." There, sadly, matters did not rest: an intrigued gentleman (then partnering Lady Bird on the dance floor) seized the fallen chemise, wondered aloud to whom it might belong, and finally deposited it in all its slippery splendor right on top of the piano.

✷ ✷ ✷

INFAMOUS FOR HER FREE COUTURE, Nancy Reagan once also gave a free peek at the size-four bod to a member of the White House Preservation Committee. Unruffled to note that her skirt had slipped to her feet when she stood to shake her guest's hand, Nancy cheerily (and probably quite accurately) informed the inadvertent voyeur that "this is one meeting you'll never forget."

✷ ✷ ✷

APPARENTLY NOT FULLY BRIEFED on the amorous habits of her boss, one White House maid extracted a sexy black silk number from between JFK's tangled sheets and took pains to make sure it was returned to Jackie. "Not my size," noted the ever-cool Mrs. K when she handed the telltale lingerie back to Jack.

GO AHEAD, BLAME IT ON WOMEN'S LIB

To this day, the reason anyone would want to replicate Lynda Johnson's wedding cake in the privacy of her own home remains a profound puzzle. Nonetheless, when the White House released the recipe pursuant to the first daughter's December 1967 marriage, there was great rejoicing in the land. But another perplexing problem soon arose: Lynda's nuptial confection, frustrated bakers complained, simply refused to rise. Presidential housekeeper Mary Kaltman, however, quickly dispatched that little mystery, along with the offensive suggestion that the White House recipe for the rather prosaic raisin pound cake was somehow flawed. "Actually, most of these women can't cook," she sniffed, "and that is the biggest basic reason why the cakes are a failure."

ALICE GLASS

✫ ✫

COQUETTE WITH A SOCIAL CONSCIENCE

A STUNNING SIX-FOOTER with long red-gold tresses and a more comprehensive collection of diamond and emerald earrings than was truly fair, Virginia socialite Alice Glass made a point of getting what she wanted. And what she wanted, in the late 1930s, was Lyndon B. Johnson. True, the gangly Texas congressman was already wed to Lady Bird; true, too, that twenty-six-year-old Glass was not only the live-in lover of wealthy publishing mogul (and LBJ mentor) Charles Marsh, but the mother of his two young children.

But such mundane matters didn't trouble Johnson's free-spirited mistress-to-be, who had boldly stolen Marsh away from his wife the very first night they met, then adamantly refused to tie the knot though he pleaded with her for years. And so, not long after she met Mr. Johnson, Glass added another boy-toy to her entourage—a rather rubish future president who proudly referred to a portion of his anatomy as "Jumbo," and was delighted to serve as her hand-picked stud.

Neither Marsh nor Johnson, naturally, was the only man to fall under Glass' sultry spell. New York society photographer Arnold Genthe deemed her "the most beautiful woman" he had ever seen, and begged for the pleasure of being buried on her estate. When she strode into a restaurant, noted another admirer, her Viking-esque splendor rendered other diners "completely silent." And nearly as dazzling as Glass's good looks was her lifestyle: at Longlea, her lavish (courtesy of Marsh) country home, original Monets and Renoirs hung on the walls, and champagne breakfasts, lazy poolside afternoons and sparkling evening salons were the rule.

Still, there was more to Glass than her money and her men. Long before the

United States entered World War II, she lamented the rise of Nazism, and made a habit of hosting Jewish refugees from Europe for as long as they cared to stay. And when newly minted naval officer Johnson spent more time posturing in front of the camera lens than he did inspecting Los Angeles shipyards in 1941, she claimed to have lost respect for his character. His physique, however, continued to exert the same powerful pull, and the still-smitten Glass bragged that her boyfriend intended to sacrifice his marriage and his political career to devote himself exclusively to her.

Sweet-talking promises notwithstanding, however, LBJ's ambitions proved stronger than his lust, and it was the long-patient Lady Bird who was at his side as he took the presidential oath in 1963. Not until a few years after that, however, did Johnson's paramour (now a divorcée many times over) completely sever ties with the president, even going so far as to burn his love letters. But as Glass herself made clear, it wasn't any sudden belated sense of propriety that set those dusty pages smoldering. It was, however, enough to make even the shameless siren of Longlea blush, or so she intimated to friends, to think that she'd ever been the bedmate of the man who was responsible for the Vietnam War.

> *"The personal is political."*
> —Ubiquitous slogan of the 1960s

LADY BIRD JOHNSON

✫ ✫

A DIFFERENT BRAND OF BEAUTY

FROM DAY ONE OF HIS 1934 MARRIAGE to Lady Bird, Lyndon B. Johnson forbade his nature-girl wife to wear flats, scolded her for snagging her stockings, and made her life miserable when she failed to use lipstick or dressed in "muley-looking" styles.

Such chauvinistic scrutiny notwithstanding, however, LBJ was scarcely ill-served by the fact that his first lady, a serious scholar who graduated in the top tenth of her University of Texas journalism class, was more of a brain than a beauty. Beddable babes, after all, are seldom in short supply for politicians of note (nor, historians suggest, for Lyndon); not so soulmates of superior intelligence and common sense. And, during the two decades while ambitious LBJ was busy blazing his path toward the presidency, Lady Bird—lauded in 1964 by *U.S. News & World Report* as a "careful, shrewd and very successful businesswoman"—quietly tended to the family coffers, parlaying her own $21,000 investment in a small Texas radio station into a $6,000,000 broadcasting empire.

Nor, as first lady from 1963 to 1969, did the fiercely independent financial whiz ("I wouldn't have a joint checking account with the Angel Gabriel," she once swore) concentrate exclusively on the famously floral aspects of her role. Instead, she prevailed on aides to tutor her on significant political issues, hosted a series of "Women-Doer Luncheons" to focus attention on female accomplishments, and allegedly lobbied her husband to amplify the Civil Rights Act of 1964 with a clause on women's equality. "What did you do for women today?" was a standard welcome-home greeting to the president from his wife.

Still, even the most assertive woman in the world couldn't help but be subtly affected by a spouse who compared females he didn't covet to cows, and once, it was alleged, rejected a superlative job applicant only because her looks weren't as outstanding as her skills. Perhaps, in fact, it was no coincidence that pleasing appearances figured so prominently in the mind of the first lady who traveled 200,000 miles across the country campaigning to "Keep America Beautiful," and patiently prodded the Highway Beautification Act of 1965 through Congress.

Keeping America beautiful

And though the vast majority of Americans (with the interesting exception of pork farmers, who loudly complained to Congress about TV spots characterizing litterbugs as "pigs") applauded Lady Bird's efforts to improve the looks of the landscape, the first lady herself apparently didn't feel she ever succeeded in sprucing up the nation to the fullest possible extent. "If I had known this was going to happen to me, I would have changed my nose and my nickname," fretted (or so the story goes) Lyndon Johnson's beautifully accomplished, ravishingly popular, and exquisitely tolerant spouse.

"Every politician should have been born an orphan
and remain a bachelor."
—LBJ

LUCI JOHNSON

✫ ✫

THE TERRIBLE TEEN

CERTAINLY LITTLE LUCI JOHNSON wasn't brought up to comport herself like a commoner. "Read all you can find in the encyclopedia about the Sudan," Lady Bird advised first daughters Luci and Lynda when they were invited to their first state dinner (honoring, of course, the president of Sudan), "and don't drink any of the wine."

Such rarefied tutelage, however, flew right out the window in the face of raging adolescent hormones. Sweet sixteen in 1963 when LBJ acceded to the Oval Office, Luci soon learned to "cuss like a trooper" (or so White House staff complained), dramatically draped a snake around her shoulders just to make sure reporters snapped her photo, and protested to the press when the president wouldn't let her meet the Beatles. Upon completing her controversial conversion to Catholicism, she promptly demonstrated her spiritual independence by throwing a beer bash for several of her favorite priests. And, of course, Miss Adolescent America was a whiz at diagnosing the personality problems of Mom and Pop: their behavior, she informed the president and first lady point-blank, was "unduly controlled and unemotional."

Then there were the boys. The male of the species, it seems, loved Luci, and she loved it right back—often in the third-floor solarium of the White House, which she refurbished as a private disco/teen trysting place. Not that dating the president's daughter was for everybody: one unfortunate University of Wisconsin student developed ulcers under the constant surveillance of the Secret Service, and was forced to sacrifice the romance to save his stomach. But when Luci took her first communion in 1965, boyfriend (later husband) Patrick Nugent and another previous steady had to share the honor of standing at her side. And like any bratty little sister, the socially active convert couldn't resist lording it over her less-outgoing older sib. "You don't need a hope chest," she taunted Lynda. "You'll never get to use it." (In turn, Lynda took to calling the boy-crazy baby of the family "Watusi Luci," and no doubt felt a little smug when she finally landed movie star George Hamilton as her steady beau.)

Though Luci would go on, of course, to face her share of uncertainties in life, her savoir faire at eighteen—when she famously dropped her "y" and replaced it with an "i"—equaled that of any know-it-all teen in the nation. Naturally, the president was startled to discover (in the pages of his daily paper) that his darling daughter had capriciously modernized the spelling of her name, and would no longer be known as sweet old-fashioned Lucy. But the cosmopolitan miss who had outgrown her own moniker would brook no criticism from old fogies like her father. "That's the world for you," she philosophically shrugged.

> *"The invention of the teenager was a mistake,*
> *in Miss Manners' opinion."*
> —Judith Martin

IF YOU CAN'T SAY SOMETHING NICE

In 1903, a grim-faced little girl named Ruth Harding, no relation to the president, was apparently cruelly tortured (perhaps with threats of ice cream deprivation, or missing the Fourth of July parade) while simultaneously sitting for her portrait by the famous painter Thomas Eakins. The result—the spitting image of a child in major pout mode—hangs in the White House today, sending a dangerous message to alienated American youth, and provoking tourists who could have just stayed home if they wanted to see a surly youngster. Even gracious Lady Bird Johnson, of all people, was once moved to remark on the girl's grumpiness to a group of visitors. But probably only once: no sooner were the words out of her mouth than an elderly gentleman spoke up in defense of poor Miss Harding—whose disposition, he noted, had vastly improved by the time he married her.

HOW RICHARD NIXON GOT THE IDEA

Discretion may be the better part of valor, but it's absolutely no fun for the audience. The media got plenty of humorous mileage, however, out of the uncensored remarks of teenager Trenny Robb regarding her White House sleepover after her brother, Charles ("Chuck") Robb, wed First Daughter Lynda Johnson in December 1967. Upon encountering the bride's restless father roaming the halls in his pajamas, Trenny told the New York Daily News, she promptly informed him that her own dad would "be in debt the rest of his life" due to the cost of Lynda's lavish rehearsal dinner. And why, indeed, should the talkative teen have attempted to conceal from LBJ the concerns she freely discussed with others? After all, Trenny revealed, the entire White House was rigged so that "everything that's said can be listened to later."

FIRST, BUT NOT FOREMOST

In the course of her thirty-two-year political career, Maine Senator Margaret Chase Smith racked up a number of fabulous firsts—first woman to serve in both houses of Congress, first woman to serve four full terms in the U.S. Senate, and first woman senator who didn't follow in the footsteps of a deceased spouse. In 1964, the sixty-six-year-old Republican also became the first woman to vie for the presidential nomination of a major political party. ("When people keep telling you that you can't do a thing, you kind of like to try it," she explained.) But there Smith's string of gender-related precedents stopped. Arizona Senator Barry Goldwater nabbed the GOP slot, and the distinction of running as the first female presidential candidate officially selected by the Republican (or Democratic) party remains up for grabs to this day.

AN ATYPICAL TEMPTRESS

Maybe it was that hard-core military image that gave one anonymous, fabulously wacko woman of the fifties the idea that Dwight D. Eisenhower might be a bondage-and-discipline sort of guy. Hoping to enlist the president's aid in resolving a land dispute, she pleaded with White House security guards for a personal audience. Finally, when her most eloquent efforts proved fruitless, she slipped a ten-pound log chain around her neck, padlocked it in place, and had the key delivered directly to Ike. But though the enticingly imprisoned petitioner marched up and down before the White House for days, Eisenhower failed to evince the slightest interest in her plight—which became considerably worse, incidentally, when it started to rain. "This method of attracting the President's attention is not recommended," noted the White House maid who recorded the incident for posterity.

JOAN CRAWFORD

✳ ✳

WHAT BECOMES A LEGEND

THOUGH COAT-HANGER QUEEN Joan Crawford was known for many things, excellent interpersonal behavior was not among them. According to her rival Bette Davis, Crawford "slept with every male star at MGM except Lassie"; Marlene Dietrich termed her "that terrible, vulgar woman with the pop eyes [who] beats her children." Still, lovely Lady Bird Johnson didn't seem to consider Crawford's reputation any reason to ban the much-dissed diva from her White House dinner honoring Supreme Court Justice William Douglas in January 1967.

Perhaps it was having to share the limelight with Douglas Fairbanks, Jr., one of the much-married movie star's numerous former husbands, that incited Crawford to new heights of bad behavior in the nation's capital. Perhaps it was some smoldering sense of rivalry with Justice Douglas, whose dizzying record in the divorce department threatened to top her own. Or perhaps it was merely the presence of Douglas' latest matrimonial prize, a wide-eyed babe of twenty-three, that pushed her primal buttons—Mommie Dearest wasn't known, after all, for her patient manner with young people.

In any event, La Crawford—who imported her own personal hairdresser to groom her for her moment of White House glory—proved to be a spectacularly ungracious (though superbly coiffed) guest. Arbitrarily dispensing with the basic elements of civilized discourse, she propositioned a gentleman at a nearby table, treated her dinner companions to an endless stream of rude remarks about the nubile new Douglas spouse (who happened to be seated just two chairs away, and was not the least bit hard of hearing), and finally lunged across her dinner partner toward Mrs. Douglas just as dessert was served, hissing, "This is the way you do it, darling!" as she abruptly removed the bewildered bride's fingerbowl.

In short, the evening turned out, thanks to Crawford's stellar bout of bad behavior, to be a smashing success. Humiliated as the hostess may have been, her unexpectedly lively little dinner certainly lingered in the memory longer than a more sedate soiree, young Mrs. Douglas managed to pick up some priceless pointers on Washington (or was it Hollywood?) protocol, and the gratified guests went away with a story they could (and no doubt would) dine out on for decades.

"If you want to see the girl next door, go next door."
—JC

A REVISIONIST EXHIBITIONIST

Only three years old when her pop was elected president in 1960, little Caroline Kennedy wasn't yet plagued by paparazzi. According to one White House staffer, in fact, the tiny first daughter once drew a crowd at her family's Hyannisport home when she performed a striptease at her bedroom window. But Caroline's days as a carefree ecdysiast were numbered: between the painfully public death of JFK in 1963 and the media's single-minded pursuit of Jackie, she quickly learned to shun the spotlight. In 1995, in fact, the former Gypsy Rose Lee of the sandbox set coauthored (with fellow attorney Ellen Alderman) *The Right to Privacy*, a scholarly exploration of what was, for at least one of the writers, a very personal topic.

EARTHA KITT

✶ ✶

CATWOMAN VS. LADY BIRD

WHEN YOU INVITE CATWOMAN TO LUNCH, you expect to see the fur fly. But somehow it never occurred to Lady Bird Johnson that entertainer Eartha Kitt (then starring as the feline female in the TV series Batman) would actually show her claws at a toney White House Women-Doers' luncheon in January 1968 to address the problem of crime.

The daughter of South Carolina sharecroppers, Kitt certainly wasn't born hobnobbing with Great Society types. "Adios, mother—," she once responded when a hotel clerk challenged her to say something in Spanish to prove her (false) claim that she was Hispanic, not black. But by the time she slid into her seat at Lady Bird's party for high-profile do-gooders, the "sultry," "sloe-eyed" (as the press invariably described her) artiste had also danced for the Royal Family in London, played Helen of Troy in Orson Welles' Parisian production of *Faust*, and once taken tea with Albert Einstein. According to Kitt, she and the seventy-five-year-old genius enjoyed a companionable chat about reincarnation (in German, one of the six languages in which she was fluent).

As Lady Bird (along with forty-nine other scandalized Women-Doers, assorted reporters and, eventually, the entire nation) would soon discover, the woman who waxed metaphysical in foreign tongues was also quite articulate in English—especially on the topic of President Johnson's failure to terminate the war in Southeast Asia. Singularly unimpressed by suggestions that planting more flowers (a uniquely Lady Bird-esque solution) and installing heavier streetlights might eradicate street crime, Kitt sprang to her feet and proposed her solution to urban unrest: an end to American involvement in Vietnam. "You send the best of this country off to be shot and maimed," she charged; no wonder "they are doing everything they possibly can to avoid being drafted"; no wonder "they rebel in the street."

Needless to say, slamming the first lady and her significant other wasn't quite the done thing among the Women-Doers, and her guest's defiantly dovish views were not again solicited by Mrs. Johnson. (Ironically, the widely reported outburst did give Lady Bird's project a boost, with 35,000 letters subsequently pouring in from citizens interested in participating in crime prevention.)

Kitt's outspoken opinions were not, however, ignored by the CIA, which subsequently opened a dossier describing her as "rude, crude, shrewd, difficult" and (here one can't help imagining the reporting agent lost in some private fantasy starring sultry, sloe-eyed Catwoman) "a sadistic, sex nymphomaniac" to boot.

> *"If Mrs. Johnson was embarrassed, that's her problem."*
> —EK

FOR BETTER OR FOR WORSE

✻ ✻

LUCI'S LOVE STORY

THE COURSE OF TRUE LOVE, as Shakespeare once observed, never did run smooth; neither, it seems, did the course of the truly big wedding bash. And while no one doubted the deep bond between First Daughter Luci Johnson and her groom Patrick Nugent, orchestrating their 1966 nuptials at Washington's National Shrine of the Immaculate Conception wasn't exactly a labor of love.

First and foremost, there was the sticky issue of how to handle gifts from politicians and foreign nations: unlike less prominent brides, the president's daughter couldn't simply accept her booty at its (preferably hefty) face value. For advice on the protocol of refusing presents, Lady Bird's press secretary turned to Alice Roosevelt Longworth, whose 1906 White House wedding reportedly resulted in an astonishing haul. "I only wish I'd gotten all those things they said I got," was the former Miss Roosevelt's helpful response.

Then nineteen-year-old Luci (a Georgetown University nursing student) thought it would be nifty to deposit her bouquet before a portrait of her profession's patron saint, a martyred maiden who was charbroiled for rejecting the advances of a Roman VIP. Alarmingly, it turned out that St. Agatha was also invariably depicted minus her bosoms (which were apparently wrenched off with pincers), and the bride's bizarre request had White House staffers running all over Washington in search of a more festive image.

Naturally, the eight-foot-tall wedding cake, looming large in the East Room, presented an array of problems ranging from the frivolous (thirteen unlucky tiers) to the fatal. Reporters were informed that the lilies of the valley topping the massive structure constituted an extra layer, and therefore they should never mention the thirteen tiers. A vigilant Department of Agriculture employee warned that lilies of the valley, if ingested, could cause memory loss and coma—and "the partaker is apt to wander about in a strange manner." Just in time, a last-minute application of plastic spray to the poisonous flora prevented any wacky perambulations among the guests.

Nor was Luci's wedding itself—an elaborate forty-two-minute ceremony attended by ten bridesmaids in eye-catching "pink-pink" frocks and seven hundred guests—devoid of unanticipated drama. Outside the Shrine, war protesters paced up and down carrying two open coffins and the sign "Wedding Rice for Starving Vietnamese—Deposit Here." Big sister Lynda fainted in her pew. And while a good time was undoubtedly had by some, White House publicists certainly never intended to reveal that Luci's bridesmaids were taught "how to sin in the car" (as opposed to the rather less stimulating news that they had learned how to sit).

And, like every bride in the world, even the privileged president's daughter—whose marriage to Mr. Nugent would endure well into the Carter administration—couldn't help feeling that events had gotten just the teensiest bit out of her control. "I wanted just my immediate family and friends," she complained as the ruckus of one of the decade's most mammoth receptions raged around her on the White House lawn. "My parents invited only the immediate nation."

"I do."
-LJ

THE STATE OF UNION

✳ ✳

RITES THAT WENT WRONG

FROM THE FIRST WHITE HOUSE NUPTIALS in 1812 (Dolley Madison's sister) to the latest in 1994 (Hillary Clinton's brother), numerous Cupid-struck couples have pledged to love, honor, and send those thank-you notes out immediately on Washington's most exclusive grounds. But apparently location isn't everything when it comes to wedding bliss…

FOLLOWING THE 1874 WHITE HOUSE MARRIAGE of First Daughter Nellie Grant, President Ulysses S. fled to the bride's boudoir, where he was later found sobbing uncontrollably. And so, it seems, he should have—Nell's groom proved to be a cad and a bounder, and the marriage did not last.

✳ ✳ ✳

ALICE WILSON, NIECE OF PRESIDENT WOODROW, didn't find her August 1918 ceremony in the Blue Room quite all that she'd expected. No offense to Uncle Woody, but she just didn't consider the historic residence particularly romantic. "Going to the White House was rather like going to grandfather's to be married," she later complained.

✳ ✳ ✳

PRESIDENT THEODORE ROOSEVELT'S DAUGHTER ALICE, whose 1906 East Room wedding to Nicholas Longworth set new standards of elegance, scored the strangest (a box of snakes) and the costliest (a $20,000 pearl necklace, compliments of Cuba) loot of any of her White House peers. More memorable still, however, were the warm farewell words of stepmother Edith Roosevelt to the departing bride. "I want you to know that I'm glad to see you leave," First Lady Edith informed the radiant newlywed. "You have never been anything but trouble."

ANOTHER VOTE FOR THE GOP

Letitia Baldrige, social secretary to Jackie Kennedy, took her high-pressure job in stride. "As long as we're not responsible for the start of World War III," she once remarked, "we're all right." A small holy war, however, was what Baldrige had on her hands when her office forwarded the wrong form letter to a priest who had invited the Kennedys to the opening of his one-man art show. Just how wrong, Baldrige learned, when the good father called to express his feelings about the note congratulating him on the birth of his son.

V

BELTWAY BABES DO THEIR
OWN LIBERATED THING

PAT NIXON

✳ ✳

THE STOIC MINORITY

A S RICHARD NIXON MADE PERFECTLY CLEAR in his notorious 1952 "Checkers" speech, mink simply wasn't in the cards for the Mrs.— a "good Republican cloth coat" would do just fine. And in 1968, when interviewer Gloria Steinem tried to get "Plastic Pat" to indulge in the luxury of self-scrutiny, the presidential candidate's wife lashed out like an angry prole- tarian mob. "I don't have time to worry about who I admire or who I identify with," she snapped. "I'm not like all you—all those people who had it easy."

To say the least. The daughter of a dirt-poor California farmer, the future first lady grew up without benefit of electricity or extensive plumbing, let alone any undue emphasis on personal psychology. And even after Richard Milhous was safely (or so, at least, it seemed) ensconced as top man in the White House, his spouse clung to her roots in the hoi polloi. "We're going to invite our friends here and not all the big shots," the fifty-six-year-old first lady assured former Nixon campaign workers at a thank-you reception in their honor. ("Of course, *all* our friends are big shots," interjected Dick posthaste.)

"I do or die," swore once-penniless Pat, to whom nothing (save, perhaps, for Richard Nixon's sudden marriage proposal the same evening they met) had ever been handed on a silver platter. "I never cancel out." And in fact, during the globe-hopping first lady's newsmaking sojourn to South Vietnam, death didn't seem like such a farfetched outcome. "I want to see some wounded Ameri- cans," she insisted, and hitched a helicopter ride to a hospital in the battle zone outside of Saigon. It wasn't her only courageous feat. On a goodwill mission to earthquake-ravaged Peru in 1970, she traveled via tiny cargo plane through the perilous Andes to personally inspect the damage. ("I didn't come here to sit," she retorted when Red Cross workers suggested she take a less active role.) Back in the States, Pat kept her cool when antiwar protesters peppered her with bits of confetti imprinted with the slogan: "If this was napalm, you would be dead." Even the ever-escalating Watergate scandal of 1972 couldn't crumble the first lady's iron-clad composure. "You all drink some champagne," she suggested sweetly when reporters tried to quiz her on the conspiracy at her own birthday party.

Plastic Pat

Still, even steel-spined Pat wasn't *quite* as qualm-free as she liked to claim. And though she stood by her man through thick and thin, the prospect of actually bunking down with the increasingly unpopular prez simply gave her the willies. "He wakes up during the night, switches on the light, speaks into his tape recorder or takes notes—it's impossible," shuddered the otherwise unflappable first lady—who, truth be told, probably shared her phobia of slipping between the sheets with RMN with millions of Americans from coast to coast. "No one could sleep in the same bed with Dick."

"I don't know what history will say about me, but I know it will say that Pat Nixon was truly a wonderful woman."
—Richard Nixon

TRICIA NIXON

★ ★

THE RETRO REBEL

IKE HER ETERNALLY UNCOOL DAD, super-square Tricia Nixon simply refused to go with the flow of the sixties thing. A girlish, defiantly well-groomed honors student of twenty-two when papa became president in 1968, Tricia preferred soda pop to Molotov cocktails, *Dr. Zhivago* to Dr. Leary, and hove close to home while her peers reveled and rioted in the streets.

Petite and overly fond of frou-frou frocks, the former class president of Finch College earned an epithet from *Women's Wear Daily* as "one of the best-dressed children in America." According to Howie Kaylan, the lead singer of the band The Turtles, his blatantly unhip hostess showed up "wearing organdy and stuff" at the White House ball where he performed. "She rustled when she walked by like a f— redwood," the turned-off Mr. Kaylan told *Rolling Stone*.

Exactly like a group of unusually well-dressed tots, Tricia and her coterie of like-minded twentysomethings enjoyed cavorting through the White House during sessions of that sophisticated party game known as "sardines," finding it most amusing to stow themselves beneath the bed in the Queen's Room. When the girl who refused to grow up wasn't playing peek-a-boo in the Executive Manse, she often disappeared for days at a time into the cocoon of her pretty pink (of course) bedroom, inspiring sister Julie to dub her "the Howard Hughes of the White House."

Even the most mundane accomplishments of the average American adult eluded (not, one suspects, altogether accidentally) Richard Nixon's pampered daughter. Not only did Tricia have no plans to bring home the bacon, she also couldn't envision frying it up. "To do it just right and not have it greasy is real gourmet cooking," she sighed. (Then again, perhaps Miss Nixon came by her opinions about those overwhelming culinary arts honestly—her father, after all, swore by a slimming diet of cottage cheese and catsup.) In any event, by 1971, when Tricia pledged her troth to Harvard law student Edward Cox in the White House Rose Garden—an exclusive 400-guest affair attended, a light drizzle notwithstanding, by Washington luminaries ranging from Ralph Nader to Martha Mitchell—she had loftier matters on her mind. "The most important thing in marriage is love, but love is so intangible," she opined obscurely.

Tricia's altared state

Meanwhile, perennial presidential guest Alice Roosevelt Longworth—whose own 1906 White House nuptials culminated her cigarette-smoking, sass-talking, gloriously unchaperoned career as the most rebellious first daughter in American history—was doing some more down-to-earth opining of her own. And as usual, Ms. Longworth saw no reason to hold her tongue when reporters tried to make the inevitable comparison between dainty Tricia's wedding and her own. "It doesn't bring back one goddamn memory," snapped the distinctly unimpressed octogenarian.

> *"[Tricia] does not like the limelight.*
> *She has a passion for privacy—like me."*
> —Richard Nixon

GRACE SLICK

WHAT TO FEED YOUR HEAD (OF STATE)

IF ONLY ACID-ROCK DIVA GRACE SLICK had succeeded in her scheme to slip Dick Nixon an LSD mickey, the paranoid, plumbing-obsessed president we remember as "Tricky" might instead have gone down in history as "Trippy."

"I was not looking to poison the guy," Slick, the Jefferson Airplane vocalist/lyricist best known for her anthems of sexual liberation and substance use, assured her biographer some years later. "That would have made him a hero like Kennedy or Lincoln. The only thing I wanted to do was show America that the guy was just not happening."

Eventually, of course, America would figure out for itself that Nixon was not the most together dude ever to inhabit the Oval Office. But if fate had smiled on Slick the day she snagged an invite to Tricia Nixon's tea party for Finch College alumnae, the realization might have come a little sooner. In any event, it's a startling testament to the hang-loose ethos of the early 1970s that subversive Slick showed up at the White House as a genuine guest, not as a war protester or a gatecrasher.

To be sure, several alarmed alumnae had lobbied to ban her from the tea, but Slick's former suite mate overruled the motion. "If there was one thing I felt sure about," recalled Mary Beth Busby, "it was that she was much too nice a girl to ever do anything nasty." (One gathers that Ms. Busby did not closely follow developments in the entertainment world.)

On the day of the great event, however, Slick threw a sop to convention and opted not to go topless, as she had once done during a performance at Gallic Park in New York. More characteristically, however, she showed up with a secret stash of powdered LSD in her pocket and a rather conspicuous escort named Abbie Hoffman who, she explained, was actually her personal body-guard.

On her own, it's just possible that Slick might have managed to pull off her psychedelic plot to doctor Dick's tea. But neither Ms. Nixon nor White House security police were eager to admit the infamous Chicago Seven defendant who had roused so much rabble at the 1968 Democratic Convention (and also nominated a pig for president). Nor were they moved by Hoffman's reluctance to leave his pal unprotected in the White House. "I understand they lose a president every three years," Hoffman protested in vain. "It's a dangerous place."

Eventually, the acid queen and the Yippie king saw that their mind-altering agenda would have to wait until another day and tripped away across the White House lawn, leaving the hostess to deliver a delightfully perverse postmortem. "If she had to come with a bodyguard I feel sorry for her," remarked Ms. Nixon, daughter of one of the most notably neurotic presidents in U.S. history. "She must be really paranoid."

"[There were] probably fifty or a hundred girls around who took eight times more acid than I did; but I wrote about it and wasn't afraid to speak about it so they nailed me as the acid queen."

—GS

BARBARA WALTERS

✵ ✵

WHEN BABA WAS BAD

JUST HOW FAR WOULD BARBARA WALTERS GO in pursuit of a story? For starters, the future "million-dollar-baby" of American broadcasting crawled on hands and knees through a dense New York crowd (scuffing, in the process, rival journalist Dan Rather's shiny new shoes) to get a gander at President-elect Richard Nixon in 1968—and, of course, to make sure she was gandered at in return. "NBC will pay," she assured Rather—incorrectly, it turned out—when her CBS competitor complained about his footwear.

Nor did Walters (who once mentioned that she would "kill myself" for an interview with Nixon) draw the line at insinuating that she considered him something of a studmuffin. "I find that he has sex appeal—he's slim and suntanned...well, he's just sexy, that's all," the *Today* show star gushed in her 1970 guide to self-assured gab, *How To Talk with Practically Anybody About Practically Anything.* And when Nixon inadvertently interrupted her interview with daughter Tricia, Walters (who, like Gloria Steinem, once posed as a Playboy bunny for a story about sexism) simply fluttered her faux lashes and suggested he join her for a photo à deux.

Not surprisingly, then, it was Walters, his apparently ardent admirer, whom Tricky Dick picked to conduct the exclusive 1971 Blue Room interview that he hoped would increase his ratings in public opinion polls. And it was Walters, too, who accompanied the president on his historic 1972 trip to the People's Republic of China—one of only three women journalists in an entourage of eighty-seven.

Long before she signed the 1976 ABC contract that made her, in one flick of the pen, both the first female coanchor ever and the highest-paid journalist in the world, the ambitious newswoman was seen on the arm of Henry Kissinger—though whether the secretary of state was a bona fide beau, or just another big name to book, only Walters knew for sure. In the midst of a rather sweaty fireside chat with H. R. Haldeman in 1971, she flirtatiously fluffed the chief of staff's cheeks with her powder puff, drawing him into such animated discussion that the special was parlayed into a headline-making three-part series. When asked if the *Today* show exploited her as a sex object, Walters would only purr, "I should hope so!"

Naturally, it crossed the less-than-charitable mind that the ace of the airwaves who, by the late 1980s, had scored face-to-faces with every newsworthy notable from Abbie Hoffinan to Anwar Sadat during the previous decade, might sometimes draw a rather blurry line between the personal and the professional. And indeed, when David Frost grilled the grande dame of the intimate TV interview on the secret of her success at ABC, she blithely confirmed his most titillating suspicions. "I worked very hard for twelve years," deadpanned Walters, "and then I slept with the producer." After Frost retrieved his jaw from the floor, the most driven woman in the broadcast business slammed her point home. If she'd actually slept her way to the top, scolded the irrepressible Baba Wawa, "do you really think...it would have taken me twelve years?"

"If you gave me a choice between the interview and the date, I would take the interview."
—BW

MARTHA MITCHELL

✳ ✳

THE SOUND AND FURY

ALEXANDER GRAHAM BELL NEVER DREAMED what havoc a woman like Martha Mitchell could wreak with a telephone. All along the Eastern seaboard in the early 1970s, slumbering reporters snapped to attention to take Madame M's late-night calls. President Richard Nixon got the blues when Martha's famous dialing finger was in a restless mood. And Attorney General John Mitchell, the Watergate conspirator who had the professional misfortune of being married to Martha, threw up his hands in despair and called her an "unguided missile."

A fiftyish blonde with a closetful of stiletto sling-backs and a political sensibility, according to friends, "slightly to the right of Attila the Hun," the wife of the newly appointed A.G. first unzipped her lip on CBS *Morning News* in 1969. "My husband," she prattled, "has said many times, some of the liberals in this country, he'd like to take them and change them for the Russian Communists." Soon thereafter, it was reported, Martha's husband also remarked that his precious chatterbox had the perfect right to say whatever she wanted—"as long as she says it in Swahili."

But the loosest tongue in the East was off and running. "She should be torn limb from limb," Martha informed reporters when a guest denounced the Vietnam War at a presidential party. "If I've got to think for him he might as well get out of the damn White House!" she fumed after Nixon allegedly claimed credit for one of her ideas. And when Arkansas Senator J. William Fulbright failed to support a Supreme Court nomination favored by her husband, the Arkansas *Gazette* received one of those talky 2:00 A.M. phone calls suggesting that someone should "crucify" the traitorous congressman. ("She is a little unrestrained in the way in which she expresses herself," Fulbright delicately observed.)

In 1973, when John Mitchell (who had resigned from the Cabinet to run Nixon's re-election campaign the previous year) was indicted on charges of blocking the federal investigation of the infamous Watergate break-in, Martha naturally raced for the receiver. "I'll be damned," she ranted to Helen Thomas of UPI, "if I'll let my husband take the rap for Mr. President. If my husband knew anything...Mr. Nixon also knew about it." As the history-making events of the succeeding months (culminating, of course, in the president's resignation) would shortly prove, the media's favorite phone freak certainly had RMN's number.

Not even Martha, however, suspected that after her death in 1976, devious Dick would actually attempt to pin the blame for the scandal that toppled him from the presidency on her, claiming that distress about her discursive ways had prevented John Mitchell from properly monitoring the re-election campaign. "If it hadn't been for Martha," he insisted, "there'd have been no Watergate." Which was, in a backhanded way, quite a tribute to the power of a woman whose one great passion was gabbing on the phone—even if Mr. President, unlike the one-and-only Martha the Mouth, was constitutionally incapable of calling it right.

> *"There's nothing wrong with America—except those jerks in Washington who're trying to run it!"*
> —MM

FROM THE MOUTH OF MARTHA

"To get along in Washington, you have to put on a false face and never let anyone know what you really think or feel."

"Anytime you get somebody marching in the streets, it's catering to revolution."

"I can't understand why the liberals are so against me. Here I am, doing their thing, trying to have some freedom of speech and they want to take it away."

"Maybe one reason that I was never taken seriously in Washington—no woman is—is it's a man's town."

"Somebody should get down and bleed for me. I try so hard."

"I've never been committed to anything…except the good of my country."

THE AFFABLE RADICAL

Back in the golden age of activism, actress/photojournalist Candice Bergen wasn't exactly a Secret Service agent's dream. By May of 1975, when the *Ladies' Home Journal* sent her to the White House for a four-day photo shoot, the future Murphy Brown had spoken out against abortion laws, protested at Alcatraz on behalf of Native Americans, and spent a spell in jail after demonstrating against the Vietnam War (in the United States Senate). Then there was her rumored relationship with nasty Jack Nicholson—a man whose knowing leer could ruin a nun's reputation—with whom she appeared in the controversial 1971 film *Carnal Knowledge.*

Nonetheless, Gerald and Betty Ford didn't seem to think their twenty-seven-year-old visitor posed a significant threat to either their security or their morality, and the session went off without a hitch, Bergen later remarking that she found the president "sincere, sensible, simple, and straight-shooting." As for her opinion of Mrs. Ford, mere words evidently did not suffice: one assumes that the former first lady took it as a belated compliment when, some thirteen years later, the producers of *Murphy Brown* made a point of depicting the surly-but-sober Murphy as an alumna of the famous Betty Ford Center.

SHIRLEY CHISHOLM

★ ★

AN AMERICAN ANOMALY

IN THIS COUNTRY," U.S. CONGRESSWOMAN Shirley Chisholm once observed, "everybody is supposed to be able to run for president, but that's never been really true. The presidency is for white males." In 1972, however, the forty-eight-year-old New York politician gleefully gave the lie to her own maxim, becoming the first black American ever to make a bid for the presidential nomination of the Democratic party. After all, explained Chisholm in *The Good Fight*, her first-person account of that precedent-setting campaign, "Someone had to do it first."

Having served since 1968 as the first black woman elected to the U.S. House of Representatives, Chisholm—a progressive feminist who campaigned for that seat under the slogan "Unbought and Unbossed"—was, fortunately, already accustomed to standing out in the crowd. "You're *what?*" exclaimed one pale, perplexed Floridian when the black female candidate introduced herself and explained that she was running for president. Ironically, however, her unique gender-race attributes often alienated the very constituencies she hoped to attract.

On the one hand, "the woman thing" (as Chisholm wryly termed a certain archaic attitude) presented a major obstacle in gaining the support of black men. "In this first serious effort of blacks for high political office," one anonymous member of the Congressional Black Caucus confided to the *Washington Post* in 1971, "it would be better if it were a man." "There she is—that little black matriarch who goes around messing things up," stage-whispered another sexist when Chisholm spoke in Chicago. "Get off my back!" the fed-up candidate finally exploded. "Black women are not here to compete or fight with you."

On the other hand, white feminists and college students, Chisholm found, often failed to understand the concerns of minorities, or why equal rights and ecology weren't her sole concerns. "I let them have it straight, too," Chisholm wrote in *The Good Fight*. "The real environmental problem is in the slums," she told a crowd of Florida students. "Let's do something about the children first, and then worry about the whales." To the final day of her campaign, Chisholm continued to mediate between her diverse groups of supporters, often explaining that "it would take women *and* blacks *and* whites and others to elect a President."

Despite the difficulties of her "killing" nine-month run (funded largely by the candidate's American Express card), however, Chisholm never considered her ultimately unsuccessful shot at the Oval Office a failure. Neither surprised nor disappointed when George McGovern got the party's nod at the Democratic national convention in July 1972, she had already made her own indelible mark on American politics. "The mere fact that a black woman dared to run for President...is what it was all about," wrote Chisholm, who would serve another eleven years in the House of Representatives before retiring in 1983. "'It can be done'; that was what I was trying to say, by doing it."

> *"My goal was to shake things up a little.*
> *I think I made a dent or two."*
> —SC

BETTY FORD

✸ ✸

TO TELL THE TRUTH

I N 1975, *TIME* MAGAZINE'S "MAN OF THE YEAR" turned out to
be eleven women. And thanks to the influence of First Lady Betty Ford
(one of the recipients of that gender-bending honor), female faces were
also popping up at an impressive rate in the Cabinet, the foreign service, and
other high-ranking government positions. "I've worked hard on my husband,"
the first lady openly admitted—though not, to her eternal regret, quite hard
enough to secure the appointment of a woman to the Supreme Court (a feminist
first that would have to wait until 1981).

Not that Betty Ford—lauded by Betty Friedan as "the best kind of liberated
woman"—was truly militant about her modern views. "Frankly, I enjoy being
a mother and I'm not about to burn my bra—I need it!" she joked. Neither,
however, was she any shrinking violet. Indeed, she even had a special White
House phone line installed so that she could personally lobby for the passage
of the ERA, prompting alarmed traditionalists to take to the streets of Washington, chanting that "Betty Ford Is Trying to Press a Second-Rate Manhood
on American Women."

But if the outspoken first lady wasn't exactly Phyllis Schlafly's best friend
(though, like the founder of Stop-ERA, Betty had raised an abundant brood),
she certainly was a breath of fresh air—and sometimes a kick in the pants—
after the secrecy and double-speak of the Watergate years. Following her radical
mastectomy in 1974, she lectured publicly on the importance of regular breast
exams, once making the down-to-earth observation that all in all, she certainly
would rather have lost a breast than her right arm. When a reporter dared to
inquire how often she slept with her husband, she cheerily replied that she did
so "as often as possible." And though the president complained that her off-

the-cuff, on-the-record remarks about abortion, marijuana, and premarital sex (none of them, in her view, capital crimes) had cost him twenty million future votes, her candor was widely applauded.

"She is too honest," wrote one *Washington Post* columnist. "[But] Mrs. Ford wears her defect like diamonds. And they dazzle." A 1976 *National Enquirer* poll revealed that the majority of its readers believed the first lady would make a better president than her husband. "If I could just get my rating up to hers," Gerald sighed.

The more-fascinating Ford.

More than a decade after his 1976 defeat to Jimmy Carter, in fact, the previous president was still living in the shadow of his more flamboyant spouse, whose much-publicized battle with the bottle led her to found the Betty Ford Center for treatment of chemical dependency in 1982. Five years later, when ABC aired a biographical drama titled *The Betty Ford Story*, reporters quizzed Gerald as to why *his* life had never been documented on TV. Having received informal instruction in feminist ideology for most of his married life, Betty's husband didn't have to think about that one for very long. "My wife is much more interesting," explained the thirty-eighth president of the United States.

*"Any woman who feels confident in herself and happy in what she
is doing is a liberated woman."*
—BF

SUSAN FORD

★ ★

THE DAUGHTER OF DUBIOUS VIRTUE

IT'S ICKY ENOUGH TO HAVE YOUR MOM speculate about your sex life, but to have the entire nation horn in on the primal act... Whatever the parameters of her purity, eighteen-year-old Susan Ford must have been mortified in August 1975 to hear that her mama was trashing her reputation all over town. If Susan was having an "affair," First Lady Betty Ford confided to Morley Safer of *60 Minutes* during a candid on-air chat, she really "wouldn't be surprised."

Maybe Mom knew more than she was letting on. Or maybe the future founder of the Betty Ford Center didn't believe that "just saying no" ran in the genes. In any event, whatever her feelings on the matter, Susan refrained from informing the media that she wouldn't be surprised if Mom was on drugs (leaving Patti Davis, who portrayed parent Nancy Reagan as a pill-popping ogre in her scathing 1992 autobiography, to pioneer the role of First-Daughter-as-Narc).

In all fairness, the media wasn't fascinated *solely* by the state of the first daughter's maidenhood. The *Washington Post*, for example, once reported that she had barged in on an Oval Office meeting with Henry Kissinger to hit the first father up for some cash. It was definitely a subject of international interest, however, when Ford showed up with some friends at a Rod Stewart concert in Washington, D.C.—an innocent excursion that the *London Daily Express* imaginatively expanded into a budding romance. (No need, apparently, for Stewart to inquire if *Susan* found him sexy.)

Other pieces hit closer to home. According to Sheila Weidenfeld, Betty Ford's press secretary, young Ms. Ford freaked when she saw the *Washington Post* photo of celebrants at her nineteenth birthday bash, among them an unnamed (but not unmarried) football player whom, she confided to Weidenfeld, she was "dating." And when the *Post* erroneously reported that she had been seen shopping with the same rogue, she was so humiliated that she nearly asked the paper to retract the piece. (Apparently Mr. Wrong had been two-timing not only his wife, but also the president's daughter—who, unlike the *other* other woman, was vacationing in California at the time of the spending spree.)

Inquiring minds will never really know, of course, whether Betty's baby girl was in fact a card-carrying member of the swinging Pepsi-and-Pill generation. We do know, however, that as a college coed in Kansas in the late 1970s, the possibly celibate (and possibly not) celebrity, who would go on to marry and divorce one of her father's Secret Service agents, couldn't snag a date to save her life. "The guys," she later recalled, "were just too scared."

> *"If the right man does not come along, there are many fates far worse. One is to have the wrong man come along."*
> —Letitia Baldrige, White House social secretary
> to Jacqueline Kennedy

ROSE MARY'S BOO BOO

Though the Watergate scandal of the 1970s shattered the nation's faith in its leaders, pink-collar heroine Rose Mary Woods emerged triumphant from the chaos. An inspiration to mediocre employees everywhere, Richard Nixon's loyal secretary inadvertently (she claimed) erased eighteen minutes of a presidential tape subpoenaed by federal prosecutors—and didn't even get fired from her job. (Instead, her boss resigned from his.) The jury is still out, however, as to whether error-prone Rose Mary was exceptionally bad—or exceptionally good—at the type of work she did for Dick.

COMMANDO COURTSHIP

Lest her courtside capers not provide adequate exercise, tennis pro Chris Evert devoted her spare time during the 1976 Virginia Slims tournament in Washington, D.C. to chasing after a local lad who caught her eye. In amour as in athletics, however, Chrissie liked to call the shots—or so the momentary object of her affections, First Son Jack Ford, was soon to learn. Far be it from the fleet-footed star to wait wistfully by the phone—instead, Evert ordered her press agent to phone a White House press agent, who in turn was ordered to order Ford to ask her on a date.

Although more accustomed to women pleading for his attention than commanding it (on occasion, patriotic young ladies even begged the president's son to autograph their lingerie), Ford eventually caved in, and the assertive champ scored her coveted face-time—demonstrating, if nothing else, that smokers weren't the only sort of women who had come a long, long way.

WHO'S AFRAID OF JULIA CHILD?

You wouldn't think that anyone would begrudge Julia Child a morsel of food. But when PBS sent Child to the White House in 1975 to shoot a play-by-play commentary on the cuisine at Gerald Ford's state dinner for Queen Elizabeth, the much-adored chef couldn't snag a sample of the royal dinner to save her life (or, for that matter, her show).

Never mind that the deal was as done as a three-minute egg, or that the camera crew was on the scene and ready to roll. When Child called in the kitchen for her tidbits from the Queen's table, the White House chef turned her down cold. "How can I tell viewers what it tastes like if I can't eat it?" demanded Child, not unreasonably. But the official order had come down from the first lady's all-powerful social secretary: "No food for Julia Child." And so the queen of TV cookery was left standing in the spotlight with her empty plate, facing the impossible task of describing a feast as sumptuous—and as invisible—as the proverbial emperor's new clothes.

BIANCA JAGGER

✹ ✹

SOME GIRLS

FOR THE NICE OLD-FASHIONED GERALD FORD FAMILY, the 1967 Summer of Love didn't actually arrive until 1975. That was the season, of course, when First Lady Betty happened to hazard the opinion—on national TV, no less—that her teenage daughter might possibly have a sex life. Too bad no one also asked for Big Betty's take on the loves of son Jack—a budding Casanova of twenty-three who was, at the moment, busy practicing his moves (or at least aspiring to practice them) on glamorous Bianca Jagger, the provocative, pouty-lipped spouse of the provocative, pouty-lipped leader of the Rolling Stones.

Or was it thirty-year-old Bianca who set out to seduce the Ford *fils* with her worldly charms? Brought up to believe "that virginity was the biggest asset in life," Mick's irrepressible Mrs. had remained as pure as the good Lord made her until the advanced age of eighteen, or so she once informed a reporter for *People*. (Virginity, one can't help noting, seems to have been a subject of extraordinary interest to the seventies media.) That priceless asset, however, had long since been squandered, allegedly on the likes of Michael Caine, Ryan O'Neal, Warren Beatty, Helmut Newton—and, somewhat less allegedly, on her lawfully wedded husband—by the time Bianca jet-setted her way into young Jack's heart.

In any event, Mrs. Jagger didn't look much like a convent girl on the day she and Andy Warhol showed up at the White House to interview her brand-new playmate for *Interview* magazine: according to the memoirs of Betty Ford's press secretary, she created quite a stir in her floppy yellow hat and matching see-through dress (what one saw through the dress, apparently, was a pair of petite lace-trimmed bloomers). Nor, as it happens, did the world-class party girl conduct herself, during her White House debut, quite like the girl next door. Instead, she complained about her bodyguards, commented that Cher spent too much money on cosmetics (meanwhile, Bianca's makeup man carried in an entire toolbox full of her facial products), and posed for an R-rated photo with Jack, deliberately placing his hand in a most provocative position.

Delightful as it might be to imagine big, bumbling Gerald Ford, the former college football star, as father-in-law to the swan of Studio 54 (one pictures some sort of domestic contretemps involving a buttered English muffin and a size-two Saint Laurent suit), a lasting relationship was, of course, simply not to be. Having enjoyed, if nothing else, a mutually publicity-generating acquaintance, the putative couple continued on very different paths. Bianca eventually renounced her high-profile lifestyle (and, presumably, her high-visibility wardrobe as well) to devote herself to various political causes in Central America. The president's son, for his part, went on to play a regular part in the popular American soap opera *The Young and the Restless*—a role which, in light of his liaison with Lady Bianca, couldn't help but seem a bit redundant.

"I don't want to be a rock-'n'-roll wife."
—BJ

ROSALYNN CARTER

✳ ✳

A NEW BREED OF BETTER HALF

BY THE TRADITIONAL STANDARDS of a Mamie or a Grace, Rosalynn Carter's innovative interpretation of her role fell somewhat short of the mark. During her four years in the White House (1977-1981), the stereotype-smashing first lady failed to designate an official Carter administration china pattern, and didn't even dent the government funds allocated to beautify the family quarters in the White House. Nor were any fashion trends ever set by the thrifty wife of a former Georgia peanut farmer: she patronized a Washington fabric store, and the conservative silk blazers she sported were often her own twenty-five-dollar-a-yard creations.

In other words, wrote Rosalynn in *First Lady from Plains*, her best-selling 1984 autobiography, "I was *determined* to be taken seriously." And so Ms. Carter, termed the "most influential First Lady since Eleanor Roosevelt" by the *New York Times*, was—first and foremost by her very egalitarian partner, Jimmy. "There is very seldom a decision that I make that I don't discuss with her, tell her my opinion and seek her advice," the president told reporters in 1979. And, he added, "on matters where her knowledge is equal to mine, she prevails most of the time."

As Jimmy was scarcely the first president to discover, not everyone agreed with his generous evaluation of his wife's acumen. "You have neither been elected by the American people nor confirmed by the Senate to discuss foreign policy," one disapproving reporter told Rosalynn in the midst of her news-making (but never repeated) 1977 sojourn to seven Central and South American countries as stand-in ambassador for her husband. And a Brazilian official was even more blunt: "Sending her down here to talk about atomic bombs and human rights is the most ridiculous thing I ever heard of."

But in other spheres, the woman the press nicknamed "The Steel Magnolia" met with more success. Due in part to her influence, an unprecedented number of high-ranking positions (three in the Cabinet, and forty-one federal judgeships) were filled by females during the Carter administration and, Rosalynn remarked, "It was always understood between us that a woman would be appointed if a vacancy occurred" on the Supreme Court. As honorary chairperson of the President's Commission on Mental Health, she testified before Congress regarding reforms in psychological services,

Dancing at the White House

and helped push through the liberal Mental Health Systems Act of 1980. And on a more global scale, she later wrote, it was her strong support that finally convinced the president to proceed with the historic Camp David meeting between Israeli Prime Minister Begin and Egyptian President Sadat that led to the Egyptian-Israeli peace treaty of 1979.

But though Rosalynn and Jimmy truly considered themselves a two-for-one team ("I'm bitter enough for both of us," she complained when Republican Ronald Reagan defeated her husband in 1981), history did not, in the end, put them on a par: a 1982 poll of presidential scholars ranked Rosalynn in third place among successful first ladies of the twentieth century—and Jimmy Carter as the least significant president save one.

"I do have definite ideas and opinions."
—RC

LILLIAN CARTER

✫ ✫

WHERE MR. JIMMY GOT THAT GRIN

LIKE SOME NINETEENTH-CENTURY BELLE, Jimmy Carter's mother thought "Miss Lillian" sounded nicer than Mrs., and took care to attire herself in something fetching whenever she ventured forth to Sunday services. But that was where the *Gone With the Wind* stuff stopped: seventy-eight when her firstborn was elected president in 1976, she smoked (a little), drank (though only in the evenings), and took great delight in almost anything "the ladies of the church think I shouldn't do." "I am a Christian but that doesn't mean I'm a long-faced square," noted Miss Lil, a resident of provincial Plains, Georgia for some sixty years.

In fact, the only kind of "square" that pertained to Lillian was the kind followed by the phrase "peg in a round hole." "I'm not in the same mold as some of the people I know," boasted the Carter family matriarch, a very independent widow since 1953. "I'm just different." Not to mention a trifle contrary: at the age of twenty-three, Jimmy's modern-minded mom defied her family by becoming a working woman, and scandalized the neighbors for several decades thereafter by providing nursing care to the black residents of Plains—and also entertaining them in her parlor. At sixty-five, she abruptly quit her job—in a convalescent home, complaining "most of the patients are younger than I." And at sixty-seven, she impulsively joined the Peace Corps, putting in a two-year tour-of-duty in a family planning clinic outside of Bombay, where she lectured about contraception, lent a hand during vasectomies, and did her damndest to overcome an aversion to lepers.

Well, probably. "I lie all the time," Lillian confessed to reporters, slyly adding that she *had* to spin the occasional whopper "to balance the family ticket." And yes, the goody-two-shoes line that the president persisted in taking annoyed his mother as much as anyone else—"I told him to quit that stuff about never telling lies and being a Christian and how he loves his wife more than the day he met her." After all, Miss Lillian primly observed, "There are some things you don't have to go around saying."

"How could Jimmy ever criticize me? I'm his mama."
—LC

QUEEN FOR A NIGHT

Just as the name implies, numerous royal visitors to the White House have indeed crawled under the covers of the antique mahogany bed in the Queen's Room—among them Elizabeth II of Great Britain and the ubiquitous Queen Mum. But the nameless young lady who shared the distinguished snooze chamber with First Son Steve Ford on the night of December 3, 1976 couldn't claim such distinguished lineage. She could, however, claim that she had picked up the president's son at a local bar—a fact to which the entire nation nearly became privy when Steve opened the door the next morning and discovered Barbara Walters and her camera crew in the hallway outside, shooting a televised tour of the White House. A brief but glorious reign concluded as quickly as it had begun: her hungover majesty was hauled posthaste out of the historical bed by last night's Romeo and sent packing down the back stairs quicker than you (or Baba) could say "Long live the Queen."

MARGARET TRUDEAU

✳ ✳

CANADA'S MOST CONSPICUOUS EXPORT

A GLOBE-TROTTING HIPPIE WITH A TWINKLE in her eye (and often, a controlled substance in her pocketbook) who wed Canada's prime minister in 1971, Margaret Trudeau wasn't the most traditional political wife the world had ever seen.

Frankly, the twentyish Mrs. Trudeau found mingling with the wizened old wives of world leaders to be a major snooze. Addressing a public audience after honeymooning with her fifty-one-year-old husband, she blurted out the first thing that came into her head: "Pierre has taught me everything I know about loving." And so often did marijuana smoke hang in the air outside her window at the prime minister's residence in Ottawa that a local police officer once dropped by with a bag of incense to help her disguise the aroma.

Some corners of the globe, however, could tolerate Margaret's unconventional brand of charm better than others. China's Premier Chou En-lai, for one, applauded her self-assurance when she sauntered through the streets of Beijing in the fall of 1973, undaunted by her ready-to-pop pregnant condition (later, she raced a reporter to the top of the Great Wall, and won). And in Cuba, Fidel Castro nearly touched off yet another international incident, flirting outrageously with the P.M.'s far-from-prim wife—who apparently flirted right back. ("I'm glad you're still with me," seethed Pierre at the conclusion of the journey. "I thought you would ask for asylum.")

Not recorded for posterity, however, were the prime minister's remarks on his spouse's uncensored demeanor during the couple's state visit to their White House counterparts, Rosalynn and Jimmy Carter. Asked by the president what she thought had become of "the student activists of your generation, and the great hippie push," Margaret proceeded to entertain her host with a riveting (if somewhat tangential) account of being strip-searched for drugs at the U.S. border, beneath a "leering" portrait of Richard Nixon that hung on the customs station wall. (She never had cared much for Nixon, it happened, since the evening in Ottawa when he talked her ear off about the sex life of his pandas.)

Soon to separate from stuffy Pierre, Margaret's exploits as a jet-setting play-mate to the Rolling Stones, Jack Nicholson, and Ryan O'Neal would continue to be a subject of equal (or, sometimes, greater) public scrutiny to her husband's role as prime minister. But when the flamboyant first lady of Canada finally consulted a psychiatrist for what she described as a persistent feeling of para-noia, the doctor could suggest no cure for what was, in his opinion, simply the condition of being Margaret Trudeau. "Everybody *is* watching you," he concluded. "That's not paranoia. That's reality."

"If you can't please everybody, please yourself."
—MT

WHAT A DIFFERENCE A DECADE MAKES

Unlike Betty Ford, who took daughter Susan's sexuality in stride, Rosalynn Carter didn't cotton to the concept of her little girl experiencing any sort of premarital *amour.* If Amy confessed she was having an affair, the very Christian Mrs. C told reporters, "I would be shocked," Of course, she pointed out, "my daughter is only eight years old."

CHER

A SCAMP, A TRAMP, AND A FAITHFUL DEMOCRAT

WHO'S SCARED OF CHER? Certainly not self-assured Rosalynn Carter, who invited the slinky actress/singer to supper on her family's very first night in the White House in 1977, and stuffed the tattooed siren full of fried chicken and corn soufflé—a rare fatty-food orgy that was, we can only assume, sweated or scalpeled away the very next day. ("She has had every kind of plastic surgery known to man," gossiped Barbara Bush, who got a good look at the anatomically improbable star at an International Craniofacial Foundation reception two administrations later.)

Under the circumstances, however, it could have been quite a risk that the first lady ran. Ultraliberal Cher, a self-professed Carter fan, raved about the president's concern for the homeless and the hungry. All-too-human Jimmy had admitted to *Playboy* magazine, just a few months previously, that he "lusted in his heart" for women to whom he was not lawfully wed. And who more lustworthy than Sonny's sexy, socially concerned ex, with those Gothic good looks, barely-there Bob Mackie gowns, and the most alluring belly button ever seen on network TV?

Nor was Cher the type to keep her libidinous longings under wraps. "Have him washed and brought to my tent," she would quip on her fortieth birthday when she first spotted hunky Rob Camilletti, the twenty-two-year-old bagel maker who was about to become the latest in a long string of December-May lovers. But back in 1977—good news for just-plain-folks Jimmy—thirty-one-year-old Cher didn't yet require her guys to look especially glam. "I've traded one short ugly guy for another," she joked when she broke off with Sonny and re-bonded with bisexual show biz mogul David Geffen.

Then again, the exotic entertainer, who listed *Ms.* founder Gloria Steinem among her buddies, probably wasn't the sort to steal Rosalynn's man without suffering some serious feminist qualms. "My friends think that you're a tight-ass and your friends think that I'm a bimbo," she once told Steinem, "so by all rights we shouldn't have anything to do with each other"—but the odd couple remained ideological colleagues anyway. And as for the president's problematic lust—well, just like so many of his *Playboy* peers, he proved to be a true Casanova only in the privacy of his imagination. ("Jimmy talks too much," snorted the first lady.)

In the end, of course, the president polished off both his post-inaugural meal and his term in office untainted by the breath of personal scandal, while Cher proceeded to burn up both the silver screen (her 1988 performance in *Moonstruck* won an Oscar) and the gossip columns with her penchant for youthful beaux. Thirteen years after that down-home dinner, however, Cher's passion for her White House pal still ran strong—albeit in a format that even his wife could endorse. Jimmy Carter, the nation's vampiest Democrat confessed to *Vanity Fair* in a 1990 interview, remained one of her true "heroes"—right up there with Michael Dukakis and Malcolm X.

> *"A girl can wait for the right man to come along, but in the meantime that still doesn't mean she can't have a wonderful time with all the wrong ones."*
> —Cher

JUDITH MARTIN

✶ ✶

TO THE MANNERS BORN

NO, *WASHINGTON POST* COLUMNIST JUDITH MARTIN (aka Miss Manners) didn't always inhabit the lofty realm of the etiquette maven, tallying up the transgressions of the socially inept, and issuing stern edicts about how to handle an insult (politely) and whether strawberries may be eaten with the fingers (absolutely not).

But even as a child, Martin apparently liked to lord it over the less uptight. "I can just see you some day wearing high-collared blouses holding a stick, tyrannizing generations of your descendants," her father once observed. And, according to the future Miss Manners, "at that minute I thought, yes, that's what I'm after. I was really born for this role."

Not that the queen of tongue-in-cheek social critique got off to a promising start. As a lowly reporter for the women's pages of the *Post*, Martin was summarily ejected from Washington's Statler hotel when the house detective discovered her loitering in the hallway, leisurely enjoying a room-service meal while she staked out an elusive interviewee. And during the paranoid presidency of Richard Nixon, the neophyte (but not abjectly fawning) newswoman was actually banned from covering White House affairs.

Looking back, however, it seems that Nixon—who certainly needed all the good press he could get—may have had his reasons for declaring Martin persona non grata. Just a few years later, after all, the once-ostracized scribe was entertaining readers nationwide with her arch commentary on the shocking state of American manners—commentary which in no way excluded the rich, the famous, or the presidential. Not even the two-centuries-old gaffes of Founding Father Thomas Jefferson, in fact, escaped the exacting eye of Miss Manners: his egalitarian "pell-mell etiquette," she once observed, led to diplomatic disaster (nobody in his White House, for example, had a clue who should go directly through the door, and who should hold it open).

Nor, incidentally, did the nation's leading expert on egregious behavior condone the penny-pinching practices of Jimmy and Rosalynn Carter, who on occasion rented out the White House to one organization or another—at a price of five to fifteen dollars a head. "Miss Manners does not mean to suggest that a president who won four years of White House residency, fair and square, does not have the right to invite whomever he wishes," conceded the self-made arbiter of correct social conduct. But under such circumstances, Miss Manners *did* suggest, the paying customer need not abide by the same genteel code that governed the bona fide guest. In fact, concluded the doyenne of democratic decorum, he or she should "feel free to mention politely any deficiencies in the establishment"—though not, perhaps, to actually make a career out of it.

> *"I made myself Miss Manners. It was like Napoleon: You crown yourself because nobody else can do it."*
> —JM

PRESS TRESPASSES

✳ ✳

TRIVIAL PURSUITS AND SHAMELESS STALKING

I N THE 1960S, HELEN THOMAS OF UPI was obsessed by the question of whether President Kennedy's puppy was in the family way. In the 1970s, Clare Crawford of *People* couldn't rest until First Son Jack Ford revealed whether he bit his nails. In the 1980s, reporters were suddenly seized by a burning need to know what brand of jelly beans the Reagans preferred, and whether Ronnie snored. But when it comes to matters presidential, the real question has always been the same: is there no depth to which a determined newshound will not sink?

DURING THE GREAT DEPRESSION, journalists despaired of overcoming First Lady Lou Hoover's longstanding prejudice against the press. Associated Press reporter Bess Furman, however, wasn't among those who succumbed to the collective funk. Small in stature but long on chutzpah, Furman squeezed into a Girl Scout uniform and managed to pass as one of the bona fide badge earners invited to a White House celebration on Christmas Eve in 1930. Needless to say, Furman's write-up of the festivities crackled with an authenticity that other reports somehow seemed to lack.

✳ ✳ ✳

SPOTTING A PREGNANT JACKIE KENNEDY at the 1956 Democratic National Convention in Chicago, *Washington Post* reporter Maxine Cheshire sidled right on up to the Massachusetts senator's wife and said a friendly hello. Even in those days, however, the future first lady wasn't crazy about the press: according to her would-be interlocutor, Mrs. K promptly "hiked up her dress and broke into a run." Cheshire chased her pregnant prey all the way to an underground parking garage, but the shy mama-to-be was remarkably fast on her feet, and the reporter never did catch up with her woman (or her story).

☆ ☆ ☆

DURING JFK'S PRESIDENTIAL CAMPAIGN OF 1960, Nan Robertson of the *New York Times* took her crack at the again-expectant Jackie. Rather than run foot races with the Democratic candidate's gravid wife, however, Robertson simply followed her into the ladies' room in New York's Commodore Hotel, leaving several male reporters glowering in the hall. Her strategy paid off in spades: in the privacy of the loo, Jackie went public on the subject of her recently reported $30,000 shopping spree. "I couldn't possibly spend that much on clothes unless I wore sable underwear," she told Robertson, who was not, of course, too modest to publish the pithy quote.

☆ ☆ ☆

AS AN AMATEUR JOURNALIST IN THE MID-1960s, First Daughter Lynda Johnson spent five days canoeing through the Canadian boundary waters on assignment for *National Geographic*. To her dismay, she was pursued every paddle stroke of the way by Marian McBride of the *Milwaukee Sentinel*, who was determined to interview the elusive "Greta Garbo of the North Woods." The celebrity canoeist finally gave in when McBride encapsulated a plea for face time in an empty liquor container and floated it down river to Lynda's camp, resulting in the historic "Bourbon Bottle Press Conference" of Nina Moose Lake.

☆ ☆ ☆

IN THE LATE 1970s, *WASHINGTON STAR* COLUMNIST Diana McClellan reported that First Daughter Amy Carter pitched a fit when she failed to win an athletic award at school, and couldn't be consoled until a Secret Service agent insisted that she receive a trophy anyway. Whether or not the item was accurate, the *Star* was subsequently flooded with angry letters from the White House (including one from Amy's disgruntled dad), and published a contrite retraction. Rather than resign in humiliation, however, canny McClellan demanded a hefty raise for all the free publicity her controversial story netted the newspaper. Reader, she got it.

PAT'S FLEETING PASSION

Though Dick proposed within hours of meeting Pat in 1938, it wasn't exactly love at first sight (or second, or third) for the twenty-six-year-old bachelorette. Nor did the dark horse candidate for her affections—who Pat continually tried to palm off on her roommate—score big points for driving her to and from her dates with other men. "I thought he was nuts or something," revealed the future Mrs. Nixon.

Some thirty-two years into her marriage when her partner was re-elected president in 1972, Pat perhaps still had reason to wonder if she'd made a mistake. Touring an athletic facility for underprivileged Los Angeles youth, a *Women's Wear Daily* reporter noted, she couldn't take her eyes off a certain hunky Junior Olympic champion. "How he got it up I'll never know," she marveled when the musclebound lad pressed an impressive 215 pounds. Of course, the first lady added thoughtfully, "I haven't seen a weightlifter in a long time."

VI

TOUGH COOKIES, HALF-BAKED
CRITIQUES, AND MUCH LATE-
TWENTIETH-CENTURY ADO
ABOUT NADA

NANCY REAGAN

✶ ✶

RONNIE'S LOADED SUBJECT

THEY CALLED HER "QUEEN NANCY." They called her "the marzipan wife." They called her "The Iron Butterfly," and even "The Evita of Santa Barbara." "Everybody was not just cuckoo about me," conceded Nancy Reagan in a 1985 interview with *Time*.

To say the least. Few armchair critics, after all, could resist dissing a designer-clad first lady who spent $900,000 on a deluxe White House makeover while her husband slashed the welfare budget and his administration suggested that catsup would do as a vegetable for the poor. "Gucci, Gucci, goo," quipped comedian Bob Hope, were surely baby Nancy's first words. And when the first lady flaunted her swanky new $200,000 china, even Joan Rivers (no slouch in the princess department herself) got in on the action, cracking that when a flying saucer landed on the White House lawn, Nancy screamed, "It's mine! It's mine!"

Lambasted for everything from her champagne tastes (one of her handbags, it was reported, cost more than the annual food stamp allowance for a family of four) to her frankly prefeminist views ("My life began when I got married"), Mrs. Reagan lamented that "virtually everything I did...was misunderstood and ridiculed." (One reason for her unpopularity, she speculated creatively, was that women resented her size-four figure, and her ease in staying slim.)

But when the high-falutin' "Belle of Rodeo Drive," on the advice of Reagan advisors, downplayed her haute couture and cultivated her latent sense of humor, she was a knockout. "I'd never wear a crown," she cracked at a New York politicians dinner in October 1981. "It would mess up my hair." As to allegations that she made her husband look "wimpish" by meddling in government affairs, she joked, "This morning I had planned to clear up U.S.-Soviet differences on intermediate-range nuclear missiles. But I decided to clean out Ronnie's sock drawer instead." Over the long haul, slamming back the one-liners (in tandem, of course, with a high-profile antidrug campaign) salvaged her sagging image: by 1985, the once-loathed first lady was ranked as one of the most popular president's wives of recent times—beating out even Jacqueline Kennedy.

Queen Nancy *sans* crown

Still, resentment smoldered on at least one side of the White House fence. "I sometimes had the feeling that if it was raining outside, it was probably my fault," complained the erstwhile Marie Antoinette of modern-day America. Of course, she also noted, "based on the press reports I read...I wouldn't have liked me either."

"For eight years I was sleeping with the president, and if that doesn't give you special access, I don't know what does."
—NR

JUST HOW NASTY WAS NANCY?

"[A]n anachronism...not only denying her earlier reality but the reality of American women today..."

—Betty Friedan

"[The Reagan] administration's number-one public relations problem."

—Lawrence Learner

"[A]n incipient Edith Wilson, unelected and unaccountable, presuming to control the actions and appointments of the executive branch."

—William Safire

"[T]he rare woman who can perform the miracle of having no interests at all..."

—Gloria Steinem

"She does not provoke; she flatters and always suppresses the little touch of the bitch inside."

—*New York* magazine

"[A] Maoist commissar advocating the extermination of flies..."

—The *Washington Post*

"Queen Nancy the Extravagant, an aloof former debutante...whose idea of hard times is tablecloths that shrink, whose doe-eyed devotion to her husband leads to hard-eyed terrorizing of her aides."

—The *Chicago Tribune*

"[A] handful...I don't think I'd want her to be my boss..."
—Son Ron Reagan

"That woman! Who on earth does she think she is?"
—Queen Elizabeth II

THE FRUGAL GOURMET

Johnny Carson quipped that her favorite snack was caviar. But back in the days before she met Ronnie, Fancy Nancy knew how to stretch a dollar. More often than not, the future first lady got extra mileage from a dinner date at the Stork Club by pocketing the leftover dinner rolls. Until, that is, the embarrassing evening when a little packet was plunked down on her table, along with a note from the owner, who wryly noted that she might enjoy some butter on her take-home bread.

EH, WHAT?

Though critics snickered at Nancy's spellbound wifely gaze, Ronald Reagan obviously took the right woman to the White House with him. Actress Jane Wyman, who signed on as Mrs. Reagan #1 in January 1940, definitely was not charmed by Ronnie's constant chatter. "If you ask Ronnie what time it is, he tells you how to make the watch," she once complained. And when Wyman (who gave her marriage to Mr. Motormouth a good nine years before calling it quits) really got her movie career going, she wouldn't give her garrulous guy the time of day. Interestingly, she perfected her Oscar-winning performance as a deaf-mute in *Johnny Belinda* by filling her ears with wax—a trick that may also have come in handy at home.

JOAN QUIGLEY

★★★★★★★★★★★★★★★★★★★★★★★★★

THE SAGE OF AQUARIUS

SHE WASN'T A CABINET MEMBER. She wasn't a high-ranking official. In fact, she only visited the White House once during Ronald Reagan's two terms in office. But for seven star-spangled years, San Francisco astrologer Joan Quigley, utterly unbeknownst to the American voters, played a vital part in shaping presidential policy and procedure.

"I was the Teflon in...the 'Teflon Presidency,'" Quigley explained matter-of-factly in *What Does Joan Say?*, her startling (and not altogether self-effacing) 1990 account of her years as celestial conduit for Ronald (Aquarius) and Nancy (Cancer) Reagan. According to Quigley, her decisive dicta regarding signs, trines, and the position of Uranus vis-à-vis the Oval Office shielded the Great Communicator from unforeseen harm, insured auspicious outcomes of speeches and journeys, and even influenced the warming of U.S./Soviet relations at the Geneva summit in November 1985. (An amicable meeting between the two superpowers, she noted, was guaranteed by the favorable relationship between Reagan's Mars and Gorbachev's Neptune on the appointed dates.)

Qualified for her occupation as State Seer on the strength of three books on astrology (one written under the pseudonym Angel Star) and several appearances on the *Merv Griffin Show*, Quigley became the official GOP guide to the cosmos in April 1981 when Nancy Reagan called to inquire whether Quigley could have predicted the January assassination attempt on President Reagan's life. In passing, the eternally misunderstood first mate also asked for some astrological assistance with a virulent bout of bad press. After all, noted Quigley, who boasted a 1947 Vassar B.A. in art history, "I knew the world quite well and understood people and how they functioned and interacted with one another, not to mention my knowledge of history and grasp of politics." Also, the first lady was "willing to pay."

Guiding the Soviets to *glasnost* was one thing; dealing with the image-conscious Mrs. R, however, quite another. Particularly galling was her indifference to the fact that Quigley charged bargain-basement fees for the privilege of serving the president. ("This was very generous of me," she pointed out in *What Does Joan Say?*). Worst of all, her cheapskate client completely downplayed Quigley's crucial role in the Reagan administration after former Chief of Staff Donald Regan spilled the occult beans in his mind-blowing 1988 memoir, *For the Record*. "This woman could chew someone up and swallow and spit out the bones and never feel a thing," the presidential prognosticator would later seethe.

But if Quigley failed to foresee Nancy's betrayal, it seems that she was nonetheless as capable of rationalizing away a petite *faux pas* as the next error-prone earthling. "I was never good at earthquakes," she shrugged when, despite her dire predictions, not even the tiniest tremor rocked her home town on the purported date of disaster. "What I do best is politics."

> *"It is awesome to be an astrologer."*
> —JQ

PATTI DAVIS

✴ ✴

THE DISILLUSIONED DAUGHTER

LIKE THE MILLIONS OF OTHER AMERICANS who never voted for Right-Wing Ronnie, Patti Davis just couldn't punch her ballot in favor of her father. An antinuclear activist who sported the slogan "One Nuclear Bomb Can Ruin Your Whole Day" on the bumper of her Toyota, Davis was frankly "frightened for the effect that my father's policies would have on the country and the world."

Equally appalling, Davis claimed in *The Way I See It*, her 1992 autobiography, was domestic policy chez Reagan. Nancy, the still-seething thirty-seven-year-old reported, rivaled Joan Crawford in the crummy mummy department, expressing her maternal instincts by scarfing down sleeping pills and slapping her daughter around. As for the Great Communicator, he wouldn't (or couldn't) hear a word against Nancy, and turned a deaf ear to Davis's pleas for help.

In fact, after Mama got done messing with her head, Davis maintained, she was forced to turn to drugs—to pay the fees of a shrink. Pushing pot, it seems, helped deal with the dysfunctional dynamics of the first family (and so, of course, did smoking it). A typical, if unusually high-profile child of the sixties, Davis also preferred funky jeans to Nancy's costly couture, fancied herself a folksinger, and didn't believe that love required a marriage license.

Unlike her less prominent peers, however, the president's freewheeling daughter also had to fit the Secret Service into her social life. On one occasion, her morning-after glow turned to gloom when she emerged from the New York hotel room of singer Kris Kristofferson, only to be confronted by three irate Secret Service agents who had spent a sleepless night on the street, waiting for her to wrap up her rendezvous. And it was no pleasure to party with comedian

Dan Akroyd when another hard-working G-man insisted on coming along for the ride.

On the other hand, being Ronald Reagan's daughter did have its perks. When Dad dropped in at her Topanga Canyon hippie pad, he just happened to mention that, as the former governor of California, he was privy to information about an imminent crackdown on local marijuana growers. Davis quickly spread the word among her more agriculturally oriented friends, with the amusing result that the president "was very popular in Topanga for the next few weeks."

Politically, however, the Gipper never did catch a clue as to what his liberal little girl was all about. On one occasion, Davis succeeded in setting up an unprecedented White House meeting between Reagan and Dr. Helen Caldicott, the outspoken Australian leader of the antinuclear coalition Physicians for Social Responsibility. But the discussion was ultimately disappointing: Reagan could not be dissuaded from his view that the disarmament movement was an evil Communist plot, and pointedly failed to shake Caldicott's hand.

It was Davis, however, who delivered the final blow to family relations, first skewering her progenitors in *Home Front*, a 1986 roman á clef that her mother termed downright "hostile," then savaging them in her acidic (though no doubt quite therapeutic) autobiography. Quoth the daughter who wouldn't have voted her father dogcatcher: "Subtlety is not a family trait."

> *"I couldn't vote for my father, I thought he was wrong on every-thing."*
> —PD

GERALDINE FERRARO

★ ★

TWO HEARTBEATS AWAY

WHILE GERALDINE FERRARO BONED UP for her make-or-break debate with Vice President George Bush in October 1984, her advisors fretted about her attire. "You need to wear something bright to stand out," one staffer suggested. But the forty-eight-year-old running mate of Democratic presidential candidate Walter Mondale thought not. "Just being a woman on that stage," she snapped, "will make me stand out."

Indeed. In theory, of course, the 1984 Democratic platform emphasized deficit control, foreign trade regulation, and the folly of incumbent President Ronald Reagan's nuclear arms policy—and not, for example, the chromosomal make-up of the nominees. In theory, too, Ferraro's most significant struggle—"coming to grips with the possibility of becoming the President" if necessary—was already behind her. But in reality, America's first female candidate for vice president on a major party ticket frequently found herself sweating bullets under a sex-specific spotlight.

For starters, she noted in her 1985 autobiography, there was the controversial bussing issue: when was a kiss just a kiss, and when was it something more? On one occasion prior to the Democratic Convention, Mondale withheld a hello smooch from San Francisco mayor Dianne Feinstein; campaign watchers concluded that Feinstein was a serious contender for his running mate. Conversely, when he planted a big wet one on Ferraro, rumors circulated that she was dead in the water. Needless to say, few male candidates had to worry about inadvertently incurring the mark of Judas.

Flowers, too, were fraught with troubling symbolism: though well-wishers often pressed bouquets upon her, the would-be V.P. scarcely wanted to "walk around looking like a bridesmaid." But if you really wanted to know what was different about campaigning as a woman, Ferraro told one reporter, it was the omnipresent threat of looking like a slattern if your slip happened to show when you raised your arm to wave. "No guy," she pointed out, "has a problem like that."

Neither, it turned out, was any guy apt to have the problem Ferraro encountered during her debate with George Bush, who repeatedly implied that the three-term congresswoman wasn't up to snuff on the *serious* issues. Far too astute to let his damaging sexist comments slide, Ferraro shot back a sharp reprimand for "your patronizing attitude that you have to teach me about foreign policy."

Only in retrospect did the unabashed (though also unsuccessful) candidate realize that when push came to shove, nearly five decades of being female might not be such a political liability after all. In fact, the entire grueling-yet-exhilarating experience resembled, in Ferraro's mind, nothing so much as rushing to the hospital to give birth. "I remember thinking to myself then, 'I wonder how I got myself into this situation,'" recalled the woman who smashed a two-hundred-year sex barrier, "and knowing I had no choice but to go in and deliver."

"Campaigns, even if you lose them, do serve a purpose. My candidacy has said the days of discrimination are numbered."
—GF

BARBARA BUSH

✷ ✷

A REALISTIC ROLE MODEL

S HE WASN'T CHIC. SHE WASN'T SLIM. She wasn't embarrassed by her wrinkles, or by stating her actual age. In short, she wasn't Nancy, and for that alone, the nation loved her.

Having Barbara Bush in the White House in the late 1980s was like kicking off a pair of too-tight shoes, or undoing the top button of your jeans after a big meal, or allowing yourself to catch forty winks in front of the TV. She had little use for the previous first lady's fancy beauty salon, though it made a fine birthing room for Millie, her dog. She liked to shake up rubberneckers by wearing an orange Ked on her left foot and a purple one on her right (complemented, of course, by several strands of absolutely artificial pearls at her throat). She was a woman who was comfortable in her sixty-three-year-old skin, and that made a huge number of her fellow (or, more to the point, gal) Americans, even those who weren't too crazy about the chief of state, feel comfortable too.

Perhaps too comfortable, according to those who thought a first lady should be a mover and a shaker, a Hillary or an Eleanor. And indeed, her pet project, literacy, was tailor-made to avoid controversy—what American, after all, would go on record as being anti-reading? True, too, that she made a point of not differing with the husband upon whom she clearly doted. Still, no adoring Nancy-esque gaze was ever fixed upon George Bush: once, his wife admitted, she had even taken up needlepoint "just to keep from looking and feeling bored to death" while listening to an oft-repeated speech.

If Barbara didn't think it politic to broadcast her personal opinions, neither did she attempt to suppress her wicked wit. "Now there's a b.s. question," she whispered when a heckler asked her husband for an explanation of his stand on abortion. "And there's a b.s. answer," she added some minutes later, as George struggled to fashion a coherent reply. And few Americans who followed the 1984 presidential race will ever forget her crack that Democratic vice-presidential candidate Geraldine Ferraro was "a four-million dollar...I can't say it but it rhymes with rich."

"My mail tells me a lot of fat, white-haired, wrinkled ladies are tickled pink," Barbara said shortly after assuming the mantle of first ladyhood, and her mail was right. Women of more recent vintage, however, thought it odd that she had dropped out of college to marry her man and

A well-grounded granny

fashioned her five-child family into a full-time career. But Barbara—wrinkles, bulges, and all—refused to think of herself as a dinosaur. "Who knows," she told graduating seniors at Wellesley College in 1990. "Somewhere out there in this audience may even be someone who will one day follow in my footsteps and preside over the White House as the president's spouse... And," she added serenely, "I wish him well."

> *"You really only have two choices; you can like what you do OR you can dislike it. I choose to like it, and what fun I've had."*
> —BB

A DOG'S LIFE

Nothing in Madam Millie's rather rambunctious White House demeanor suggested a latent literary talent: she seldom walked when she could run, put her feet up on the furniture, and sometimes killed squirrels on the lawn just for sport. But when Millie sat down to write her memoirs in 1990, the result was a rapid-fire bestseller that netted nearly $800,000 in royalties in its first year—a sum that far exceeded the annual salary of the president. Still, the accomplished auteur wasn't to be a rich bitch for long: ghostwriter Barbara Bush turned over every cent of the windfall from *Millie's Book* to her Foundation for Family Literacy, leaving the now-famous first dog to lope away with her tail between her legs.

OVEREXPOSURE

Silk or cotton? Lace-trimmed or plain? Sad to say, the world will never know exactly what sort of intimate apparel model Jill Goodacre slipped into for her supper with George and Barbara Bush. On the other hand, the underpinnings of Goodacre's relationship with musician Harry Connick, Jr. were definitely looking a little frayed. Discovering that Goodacre hadn't been designated as his dinner partner, the artiste pouted, glowered, and even threatened not to perform as planned. As to what triggered the ugly tantrum, goodness only knows—after all, it wasn't as though every guy in the dining room didn't already have a crystal clear image of what Connick's date, the dishy Venus of the Victoria's Secret catalog, looked like in her skivvies.

BABES ON THE BRAIN

In the year 1992, one might like to think that the vice president of the United States had more pressing matters on his mind than the reproductive system of a TV sitcom character. But when SWF Murphy Brown had a baby, Dan Quayle had a cow. Never mind that the gruff media star was an entirely fictitious character: her failure to obtain a marriage license before going into labor (or, for that matter, the boudoir) threatened the nation's most "basic values." Not only that, Quayle railed in his headline-making speech, but manless Murphy also "mock[ed] the importance of fathers by bearing a child alone and calling it just another life-style choice."

Four years later, Quayle was still trying to backpedal from the furor that diatribe caused. "To the extent that my remarks were taken as criticism of single mothers," he reinterpreted, "I was certainly misunderstood. If anything, I was trying to be their champion."

Somehow, it's hard to imagine that baby bliss would soften Murphy's brain—or that of any other solo mom—enough to buy that one.

PEGGY NOONAN

✮ ✮

THE TALENT BEHIND THE TALKING HEAD

"T HE BOYS OF POINTE DU HOC"; "a thousand points of light"; "a kinder, gentler nation…" As ghostwriter for the Great Communicator Ronald Reagan and on-call bard to George H. Bush, Peggy Noonan personally penned many of the most inspired phrases by which history will remember the fortieth and forty-first presidents of the United States.

Spinning out the soundbites that mesmerized the nation (and made the boss look good), however, wasn't quite the dream job that Republican wordsmith Noonan—a former writer and producer for CBS News—might have hoped. True, few other former English majors pulled down a paycheck reading great poetry for inspiration, or poring over the Gettysburg Address. Nor was the nation's first celebrity speechwriter averse to basking in her glory. ("Whenever she wrote a good line," complained one colleague, "she got up and held a press conference.")

But coping with the macho of the men in the White House, Noonan found, was enough to give Virginia Woolf writer's block. Stuffy "Harvardheads" from the State Department sauntered into her office with clunky policy statements to slip into her speeches, and stayed to pontificate on their superior grasp of English literature. (A knowing remark regarding Ezra Pound, however, could work wonders—"If you dropped the right cultural references they'd realize it might not work if they patronized you.") Rampant "testosterone poisoning" once inspired several Bush aides to argue that the word "gentler" had no place in a truly manly acceptance speech; one associate suggested that Noonan wasn't qualified to write Reagan's now-famous remarks commemorating the fortieth anniversary of D-Day because "you haven't been in the service…and you don't know what it's like to fight."

Then there was the perpetual battle to stay in the sandbox with the big boys, despite Nancy Reagan's efforts to steal her husband's star speechwriter away. In desperation, Noonan deliberately churned out insipid commentary for the boss's wife ("My life didn't begin until I met Ronnie…"), which only endeared her to Nancy all the more. Fortunately, a face-to-face meeting was less propitious, and the first lady—or so Noonan claimed—literally curled her lip when she noticed the writer's wrinkled khaki skirt. (After that, when Noonan saw Nancy coming, she ducked behind a pillar.)

Looking back on her exhilarating, exasperating Washington career, Noonan (who retired from the political scene in 1989 to write a memoir of her White House years) offered some sage advice to her successors in the bastion of patriarchal power: "Don't fall in love with politicians, they're all a disappointment. They can't help it, they just are." And, as the nation's foremost authority on pithy presidential words once advised another speechwriter: "Speak softly but carry a big Bic."

"A great speech is literature."
—PN

HILLARY CLINTON

✳ ✳

SHE ~~COULDA BEEN~~ WAS A CONTENDER

BUY ONE, GET ONE FOR FREE," suggested Bill Clinton, the 1992 presidential hopeful either saddled or blessed, depending how you looked at it, with a whip-smart lawyer wife who couldn't quite part with her own last name. But after the deal went down, it seemed, no one knew quite what to make of the formidable new first lady, despite the assurances of *Family Circle* magazine that Yale J.D. Hillary Rodham Clinton mixed up an even tastier batch of chocolate chip cookies than her Republican counterpart, career homemaker Barbara Bush.

When the president appointed his wife to head his much-ballyhooed national commission on health-care reform, for example, many Americans reacted as though the two-for-one first lady had blasted her way into the Oval Office with an Uzi and set up shop as czar. (In fact, it was the media that dubbed Mrs. Clinton "Empress Hillary.") However, flashing her femme side didn't render the "Lady Macbeth of Little Rock" any more lovable—a series of glamour shots in the December 1993 issue of *Vogue* was widely disparaged as inappropriate and demeaning to professional women. ("A false feminist," pronounced one writer for *The New Republic*.)

Then came Whitewater, a veritable Pandora's box of convoluted cover-up scandals about the Clinton finances (historically managed by Hillary) that seemed, to the non-Republican eye, just about as synthetic as polyester, and as little prone to spontaneous shrinkage. A plethora of Senate hearings, subpoenaed testimony, and federal investigations notwithstanding (not to mention William Safire's notorious characterization of the first lady as a "congenital liar"), nobody could quite put a finger on what, exactly, Hillary had done wrong. Perhaps *Washington Post* writer Sally Quinn wasn't far off the mark.

"There's just something about her," wrote Quinn, "that pisses people off."

With Hillary at the helm, the old American sport of below-the-belt first lady-baiting enjoyed a new revival. Rumors circulated that the celebrated children's rights advocate (allegedly a rabid Marxist) had lobbed a lamp at Bill in a fit of pique, been discovered in flagrante delicto with another woman, and that suicided White House aide Vincent Foster had been her secret lover. "A scumbag, a hand job, and knife-in-the-back Babbitt," frothed one New York weekly.

Hillary holds her own

When the forty-eight-year-old first lady spoke wistfully of wanting another child, cynics sneered that she was angling for the 1996 vote of the family values crowd. Yet her popularity ratings soared when Bill belatedly confessed his bad-boy behavior with intern Monica Lewinsky—apparently the public found Hillary more palatable in the role of victim. Still, some blamed her "cold," "emasculating" nature for the lapse, while others blasted her for not divorcing him on the spot.

And then came Chapter Two. Liberated at the conclusion of Bill's second term from the chimerical role of first lady, Hillary burst upon the political scene as a formidable political force in her own right. In 2000, New York voters—curiously unperturbed by Hillary's "cold" persona or unabashed drive to power—elected her to represent them in the United States Senate. In 2004, they resoundingly returned her to office for a second term. And in 2007, she announced herself as a contender for the 2008 Democratic presidential nomination. "I'm in, and I'm in to win," she proclaimed.

It was an unprecedented moment in American politics, and a long-awaited triumph for the "sisterhood of the traveling pantsuits," as Hillary (riffing on both her own sartorial preference and the bestselling young adult series, *Sisterhood of the Traveling Pants*) referred to her broad base of supporters. An anomaly as the female frontrunner for a major party's nomination, Hillary was also surely the only aspiring nominee ever slammed as "uppity," a "Mama," and a "stripteaser," or lambasted for revealing a hint of cleavage in a televised speech. "In the end," countered columnist Ellen Goodman, decrying the boob-ish brouhaha, "the question is not whether a candidate can show a hint of breast but whether you can have breasts and be president."

The question remained unanswered. After a grueling, hard-fought race, in which Hillary prevailed in more primaries and caucuses than any woman in U.S. history, sudden superstar Barack Obama nabbed the nomination, and his rival reluctantly bowed out. Never one to burn bridges behind her, though, Hillary managed to put a positive spin on the loss. "Although we weren't able to shatter that highest, hardest glass ceiling this time," she told her backers in a moving, masterfully-crafted concession speech, "thanks to you, it's got about eighteen million cracks in it."

Stay tuned.

"In the Bible it says they asked Jesus how many times you should forgive, and he said seventy times seven. Well, I want you all to know that I'm keeping a chart."
—HC

SO IS THAT WHAT THEY MEAN BY "INTERNAL AFFAIRS"?

Hired in 1995 as a White House intern, twenty-one-year-old Monica Lewinsky developed an instant crush on über-boss Bill Clinton. She didn't have to work hard to get his attention. After a few friendly public encounters, she hiked up her jacket in back to flaunt her thong-style underwear, and he took the bait.

Let's just say the affair could have been more romantic. No dancing, no candlelit dinners, no kissing on the beach. It was all about chance encounters in the midst of long days (and nights) of work. Clinton took phone calls from members of Congress while Lewinsky bestowed him with sexual favors. He refused to go all the way. And he didn't even notice the telltale stain on Lewinsky's coat-style navy-blue size-twelve dress from the Gap.

Confronted with rumors of the affair, Clinton swore, under oath, that he and Lewinsky were not romantically linked. But then Lewinsky's former coworker, Linda Tripp, went public with a recording of Lewinsky bubbling and babbling about the affair. When Clinton finally confessed to an "inappropriate relationship," the House of Representatives impeached him for perjury. A U.S. Senate trial ensued, and Clinton was ultimately acquitted.

Sadder, wiser, and much more famous, Lewinsky went on to serve as a Jenny Craig spokesperson, briefly host a TV reality show, design handbooks, and receive a Master's degree from the London School of Economics.

TALK ABOUT THROWING
YOUR WEIGHT AROUND

Born in Czechoslovakia in 1937, Madeleine Albright "fell in love with Americans in uniform" as a child in war-torn Europe. "And," she writes, "I continue to have that love affair." Some sixty years later, when President Bill Clinton appointed her U.S. secretary of state, America returned the compliment. The first woman ever to head the State Department, Albright had not only studied the lessons of World War II, but also personally experienced them. As a result, she kept a vigilant eye out for human rights abuses, and unabashedly advocated the use of "force against force." "What's the point of you saving this superb military, Colin, if we can't use it?" Albright scolded her successor, Colin Powell, when he was reluctant to play the heavy. Ever the diplomat, Albright endorsed Hillary Clinton's campaign for the Democratic presidential nomination in 2008, but also has served as a foreign policy advisor to Clinton's rival, President Obama. A prolific author of "think pieces" and letters offering unsolicited advice to world leaders, the diminutive diplomat claims to leg press an astonishing 400 pounds.

VII

AND SO IT GOES

✳ ✳

I'D RATHER BE READING

"George and I are complete opposites," Laura Bush once proclaimed. "I'm quiet, he's talkative, I'm introverted, he's extroverted"—and, she noted slyly, "I can pronounce 'nuclear.'" (The forty-third U.S. president, despite his Yale pedigree, consistently butchered the word.) As to whether their political views likewise diverged—well, who knew? The literate first lady, a former schoolteacher and librarian, a woman with a deep feeling for Dostoevsky's *The Brothers Karamazov*, was rumored to harbor a liberal tendency or two. Once, she had even ventured that *Roe vs. Wade*, the Supreme Court's 1973 decision legalizing abortion, should not be overturned. Her non-vetted views on most topics, however, went unexpressed. "If I differ with my husband, I'm not going to tell you about it—sorry," she repeatedly told reporters.

And a good thing, too, per G.W. "She stays out of the limelight," he remarked approvingly. As it happened, though, Mrs. Bush had already experienced an indelible moment of tragedy-infused fame at the age of seventeen, when she ran a stop sign and collided with another car. The other driver, a classmate, died instantly. While she seldom spoke of the painful subject, one imagines that the incident garnered her enough unsolicited attention to last a lifetime.

In fact, when Laura agreed to marry George after their whirlwind three-month courtship in 1977, it was on the condition that he never ask her to make a campaign speech. And when new mother-in-law Barbara politely inquired about Laura's interests, a passion for politics was not among them. "I read and I smoke," she said, effectively curtailing the discussion. But as a member-by-marriage of the Bush political dynasty (father-in-law George H., of course, would occupy the White House from 1989 through 1992), Laura's preferences were apparently moot. The day after the wedding, the couple hit the campaign trail together, although not with great success—the bride, it was noted, lapsed into nervous silence when speechifying, and the groom did not, in the end, go to Congress. During Bush's two subsequent bids for the Texas governorship, however, Laura grew increasingly more loquacious, if not more vocal about her personal views. And in 2000, she even agreed to deliver the keynote address of the 2000 GOP convention. "One day, God willing, George will be a fabulous grandfather," she said, concluding her well-received remarks (and telegraphing her own non political priorities). "In the meantime, he'll make a great president."

Low-key Laura

As first lady, Laura devoted herself to promoting literacy and women's health issues domestically and abroad, and distinguished herself as the first person other than a president to deliver the weekly presidential radio address (her topic: the challenges facing Afghani women during the U.S. invasion of that country). And, as Bush's increasingly unpopular—and, many Americans felt, unnecessary—Iraqi war ground on, pollsters consistently found that that the first lady's public approval ratings soared far above the president's.

"Though my plans at the moment are vague, I can assure you that I'll never run for the Senate in New York," Laura quipped, ribbing predecessor Hillary Clinton, as her stint in the White House drew to a close. She spoke of involvement with the George Bush Presidential Library in Texas, and of continuing work on behalf of literacy issues. Whether such efforts might include finally teaching her husband how to pronounce "nuclear" (nü-klē-ər), she did not say.

"It's not easy when your husband runs for president."
—LB

CONDOLEEZZA RICE

★ ★

NEOCONDI

Condoleezza Rice intended to become a concert pianist, not secretary of state. Her parents named her with Italian opera in mind; Condoleezza is derived from the stage direction "with sweetness." A musical prodigy, she was accepted as a freshman at the University of Denver at the age of fifteen, planning to devote herself to art. By nineteen, however, Rice had earned a B.A. in political science, and music was merely an avocation. Swept off her feet by the intellectual prowess of poli-sci professor Josef Korbel, father of Madeleine Albright (herself secretary of state from 1997 to 2001), the teen took Korbel's advice and changed her major to international studies. All for the best, apparently: frankly, Rice concluded at the time, she didn't have the chops to succeed as a solvent musician. She did, however, step onto the world stage, no piano needed.

Rice went on to make a name for herself as a teacher at Stanford University (during which time she switched her party allegiance, becoming a devout Republican), consult with the Pentagon and George Herbert Bush as a foreign affairs expert, and serve as national security advisor under George W. Bush from 2001 to 2005. In 2005, at the outset of Bush's second term, Rice was named secretary of state—the second woman, and the only African-American woman, ever appointed to that position.

A secretary of steely elegance, Rice appeared to indulge herself only in a slight obsession with pigskin and a fetish for footwear while in the public eye. In 2005, doing diplomacy in black stiletto boots and a skinny mini, she set the German media abuzz. That was nothing, however, to the tsunami of bad press she received later that year when caught shopping for thousand-dollar Italian shoes in Manhattan—at the height of the New Orleans flooding crisis. Queried about her post-secretarial plans, Rice hinted that she might enjoy an assignment as football commissioner.

Childless and, by all accounts, unencumbered by a partner of either sex (though at one Washington dinner party, she accidentally referred to George W. Bush as "my husband"), the hawkish secretary of state, who performed with world-renowned cellist Yo-Yo Ma in 2002, found time during her top-level tenure to play in a chamber group. Among her favorite compositions: Mozart's Piano Concerto in D Minor, Mussorgsky's "Boris Godunov," and the Aretha Franklin anthem "Respect".

> *"My parents had me absolutely convinced that, well, you may not be able to have a hamburger at Woolworth's but you can be President of the United States."*
> —CR

MARY CHENEY

★ ★

DIFFERENT DAUGHTER

According to Mary Cheney, the second daughter of former Vice President Dick Cheney, "it wasn't a secret that I was gay. I'd come out to my parents during my junior year of high school on the day that I also wrecked the family car." Despite being out, however, Cheney—a former gay and lesbian outreach coordinator for the Coors Brewing Company, and the director of vice presidential operations for the Bush-Cheney 2004 Presidential re-election campaign—did not feel compelled to notify each and every American of her sexual orientation, or the fact that her life partner did not have a penis. On the other hand, Mary's mother, Second Lady Lynne Cheney, overtly worked both sides of the Sapphic aisle. While Mama Cheney's 1981 novel, *Sisters*, featured a love affair between ladies, she adamantly denied her daughter's lesbianism on national television in 2001. Later, she flip-flopped once again, publicly proclaiming her opposition to any Constitutional amendment banning same-sex marriage.

A little earlier in history, or maybe much later, Cheney's sexuality might have been a matter of minimal public interest. But in 2004, the Bush administration strongly supported the proposed Federal Marriage Amendment to the Constitution, a provision limiting marriage and related rights strictly to male-female pairs. So which would Cheney's papa choose: allegiance to the Bushites or the best interests of his daughter? (And for that matter, how could Cheney herself tolerate the position of the party that employed her?) Either way, Vice President Cheney was bound to look like a hypocrite, a fact not lost on John Kerry, the Democrat's candidate for president in 2004, and John Edwards, their would-be VP. Both Johns, during the course of pre-election debates, slyly managed to mention the lesbianism of their opponent's thirty-five-year-old offspring.

"I'd rather not be known as the Vice President's lesbian daughter," said Cheney, who has since published a memoir (*Now It's My Turn*), given birth to her first child, and after a brief bonding-with-baby hiatus, returned to work for a lobbying/campaign management firm. But of course "the Vice President's lesbian daughter" is precisely how most Americans think of her today.

"Having loving and supporting parents didn't make me feel any better about the possibility of seeing my personal life splashed across newspapers and tabloids."
—MC

SARAH PALIN

✳ ✳

THE CURIOUS CAMPAIGN OF "CARIBOU BARBIE"

Let no one declare Sarah Palin, the Republicans' vice presidential nominee of 2008, a personage of no distinction. A beauty pageant contestant, an ass-kicking athlete, a girl who enjoyed getting in a little moose hunting before school—need one say more? Well, yes, one does: Palin stands alone as the only woman would-be Veep to personally kill a moose, field-dress it, and proudly display its rack in her home.

Elected mayor of Wasilla, a tiny exurb of Anchorage, in 1996, the ambitious Alaskan next set her sights on the governorship, which she bagged in 2006. Impressed by her moxie (and badly in need of an outspoken pro-life candidate), the Republicans tapped the hitherto obscure pol as running mate for John McCain in his presidential campaign of 2008. Oops! Folksy, unaffected, and often downright unintelligible, Palin momentarily captured the affections of the "Joe Six-Pack" voting base (as she dubbed her anti-elitist, just-folks supporters). But the love fest soured as Palin's image as a straight-shooter began to shatter, and she emerged as the proverbial loose cannon. For one thing, her spending habits weren't quite as working class as her rhetoric. Outed on *The Huffington Post* blog as a "Neiman Marxist," Palin was revealed to have squandered over $150,000 worth of campaign funds on *haute couture*, luggage, and jewelry for herself and her burgeoning family tribe (which included several children, a pregnant teen, a baby with Down syndrome, and house-hubby Todd Palin, whose own claim to fame was as four-time winner of the world's longest snow-machine race). Increasingly disgruntled, McCain staffers let loose a volley of shocking leaks. It was reported that Palin, running late for a meeting in her hotel room at the GOP convention, wore nothing but a towel when she greeted the two male aides who were to brief her. Staffers complained of her refusal to receive pre-interview coaching and her tearful rages over the resulting bad press. And damning terms like "whack job" and "diva" were bandied about—not by Democrats, but by Palin's fellow Republicans.

Questioned, after the Democratic triumph in November 2008, about plans to seek the presidency in 2012, the volatile non-Veep made what just may have been the most sensible remark of her entire campaign. "We'll see what happens then," she conceded. At the moment, though, 2012 certainly seemed "a long way off."

Just your average Alaskan

"There's a place in Hell reserved for women who don't support other women."
−SP

MICHELLE OBAMA

✱ ✱

"BARACK'S ROCK"

When Michelle LaVaughn Robinson and Barack Obama met in the summer of 1989, she was clearly the Alpha of the pair. A newly-fledged corporate lawyer at the Chicago law firm of Sidley Austin, she had been assigned as advisor to the twenty-eight-year-old summer associate from Harvard Law School, her own alma mater. Not only did the newcomer have a "strange name," but, the future first lady predicted, "any black guy who spent his formative years on an island had to be a little nerdy, a little strange." Barack, the blushing Beta, fell for his mentor immediately. But she didn't budge for a month, refusing date after date before she consented to the classic dinner-and-movie deal (and let the record show that the legal beagles took in Spike Lee's *Do The Right Thing* on that historic evening.) When the future president thanked director Spike Lee for the success of this first date, Lee replied, "Well, it's a good thing you didn't see *Driving Miss Daisy*!"

In 1992, the power couple tied the knot, the bride now pursuing a public policy career. Over the next decade, she gave birth to two daughters, Malia and Sasha, snagged a prestigious post (and a six-figure salary that exceeded her husband's not-insignificant earnings) as Vice President for Community and External Affairs at the University of Chicago Hospitals, and grudgingly agreed to campaign for Barack during his 2000 run for the U.S. House of Representatives. (The only thing she enjoyed about campaigning, she said at the time, was seeing so many people's living rooms, and getting ideas for how to decorate her own.)

Picture perfect on the campaign trail for her husband's historic presidential campaign, Ms. Obama appeared on the "Best Dressed" lists of several prominent publications, including *Vanity Fair* and *People*. Her straightforward verbal style, however, did not always meet the same degree of approbation as her elegant, streamlined ensembles. When she remarked that her husband's nomination had made her proud of her country "for the first time in my life," patriotic types went ballistic. "An angry black woman," one Fox commentator sneered. On the other hand, when she aired her wifely gripes in public—the would-be president, it seemed, left his socks lying around the house, forgot to put the butter away, and suffered from terrible morning breath—her popularity ratings soared. And, presumably, with no backlash from Barack.

Michelle, *Ma belle*

"We have a rule in our house that I can tease and he can't," she notes.

It's de rigueur, of course, for politicians to praise their spouse's unwavering support, and Obama has received her share of husbandly accolades. Not only is the first lady all that, but, Obama says, "She is the best Hula-Hooper I know."

"You are a good man, but you are still a man."
—MO (to her husband)

Allen, Gracie. *How to Become President*. New York: Duell, Sloan and Pearce, 1940.

Andersen, Christopher. *Jack and Jackie: Portrait of an American Marriage*. New York: William Morrow and Company, Inc., 1996.

Anthony, Carl Sferrazza. *First Ladies*. Vol. I. New York: William Morrow and Company, Inc., 1990.

———. *First Ladies*. Vol. II. New York: William Morrow and Company, Inc., 1991.

Baldrige, Letitia. *Of Diamonds and Diplomats*. Boston: Houghton Mifflin Company, 1968.

Blashfield, Jean F. *Hellraisers, Heroines, and Holy Women*. New York: St. Martin's Press, 1981.

Bly, Nellie. *The Kennedy Men*. New York: Kensington Books, 1996.

Boller, Paul F., Jr. *Presidential Wives*. New York: Oxford University Press, 1988.

Brodie, Fawn M. *Thomas Jefferson*. New York: WW. Norton & Company, Inc., 1974.

Bryant, Traphes, and Frances Spatz Leighton. *Dog Days at the White House*. New York: Macmillan Publishing Co., Inc., 1975.

Bush, Barbara. *Barbara Bush: A Memoir*. New York: St. Martin's Press, 1994.

Caro, Robert A. *The Years of Lyndon Johnson: Means of Ascent*. New York: Alfred A. Knopf, Inc., 1990.

———. *The Years of Lyndon Johnson: The Path to Power*. New York: Random House, Inc., 1983.

Caroli, Betty Boyd. *First Ladies*. New York: Oxford University Press, 1995.

Carpenter, Liz. *Ruffles and Flourishes*. Garden City, New York: Doubleday & Company, Inc., 1970.

Carter, Rosalynn. *First Lady from Plains*. Boston: Houghton Mifflin Company, 1984.

Chisholm, Shirley. *The Good Fight*. New York: G. P. Putnam's Sons, 1992.

Davis, Patti. *The Way I See It*. New York: G. P. Putnam's Sons, 1992.

DeGregorio, William A. *The Complete Book of U. S. Presidents*. New York: Barricade Books Inc., 1993.

Edmondson, Madeleine, and Alden Duer Cohen. *Women of Watergate*. New York: Stein & Day, 1975.

Exner, Judith Katherine, and Ovid Demaris. *My Story*. New York: Grove Press, Inc., 1977.

Faber, Doris. *The Life of Lorena Hickok*. New York: William Morrow and Company, 1980.

———. *The Mothers of American Presidents*. New York: The New American Library, Inc., 1968.

Faderman, Lillian. *Odd Girls and Twilight Lovers*. New York: Columbia University Press, 1991.

Fadiman, Clifton, ed. *The Little, Brown Book of Anecdotes*. Boston: Little, Brown and Company, 1985.

Ferraro, Geraldine A., and Linda Bird Francke. *Ferraro: My Story*. New York: Bantam Books, Inc., 1985.

Heymann, C. David. *A Woman Named Jackie*. New York: Penguin Books USA Inc., 1990.

Hickok, Lorena A. *Eleanor Roosevelt: Reluctant First Lady.* New York: Dodd, Mead & Company, 1962.

Hoyt, Ken, and Frances Spatz Leighton. *Drunk Before Noon: The Behind-the-Scenes Story of the Washington Press Corps.* Englewood Cliffs, New Jersey: Prentice-Hall, Inc., 1979.

James, Edward T., Janet Wilson James and Paul S. Boyer, eds. *Notable American Women 1607-1950.* Cambridge, Massachusetts: Belknap Press, 1971.

Jeffries, Ona Griffin. *In and Out of the White House.* New York: Wilfred Funk, Inc., 1960.

Jensen, Amy La Follette. *The White House and Its Thirty-Five Families.* New York: McGraw Hill, 1970.

Lash, Joseph P. *Eleanor and Franklin.* New York: W.W. Norton & Company, Inc., 1971.

McHenry, Robert, ed. *Famous American Women.* New York: Dover Publications, Inc., 1980.

McLellan, Diana. *Ear on Washington.* New York: Arbor House Publishing Company, 1982.

McLendon, Winzola, and Scottie Smith. *Don't Quote Me!* New York: E. P. Dutton & Co., Inc., 1970.

Mappen, Marc. *Murder and Spies, Lovers and Lies.* New York: Avon Books, 1996.

Martin, Mart. *Did She or Didn't She? Behind the Bedroom Doors of 201 Famous Women.* New York: Citadel Press, 1996.

Mayo, Edith P., ed. *The Smithsonian Book of the First Ladies.* New York: Henry Holt and Company, 1996.

Miller, John Chester. *The Wolf by the Ears: Thomas Jefferson and Slavery.* New York: Macmillan Publishing Co., Inc., 1977.

Morgan, Kay Summersby. *Past Forgetting: My Love Affair with Dwight D. Eisenhower.* New York: Simon and Schuster, 1976.

Noonan, Peggy. *What I Saw at the Revolution: A Political Life in the Reagan Era.* New York: Random House, Inc., 1990.

Oppenheimer, Jerry. *Barbara Walters: An Unauthorized Biography.* New York: St. Martin's Press, 1990.

Parks, Lillian Rogers, and Frances Spatz Leighton. *My Thirty Years Backstairs at the White House.* New York: Fleet Publishing Corporation, 1961.

Quigley, Joan: *What Does Joan Say? My Seven Years As White House Astrologer to Nancy and Ronald Reagan.* New York: Carol Publishing Group, 1990.

Quirk, Lawrence J. *Totally Uninhibited: The Life and Wild Times of Cher.* New York: William Morrow and Company, Inc. 1991.

Read, Phyllis J., and Bernard L. Witlieb. *The Book of Women's Firsts.* New York: Random House, Inc., 1992.

Rowes, Barbara. *Grace Slick.* Garden City, New York: Doubleday & Company, Inc., 1980.

Reagan, Nancy. *My Turn.* New York: Random House, Inc., 1989.

Sicherman, Barbara, and Carol Hurd Green, eds. *Notable American Women: The Modern Period.* Cambridge, Massachusetts: Radcliffe College, 1980.

Smith, Marie, and Louise Durbin. *White House Brides.* Washington, D.C.: Acropolis Books, 1966.

Tartan, Beth, and Rudy Hayes. *Miss Lillian and Friends: The Plains, Georgia, Family Philosophy and Recipe Book.* New York: A & W Publishers, 1977.

Teichmann, Howard. *Alice: The Life and Times of Alice Roosevelt Longworth.* Englewood Cliffs, New Jersey: Prentice-Hall, Inc., 1979.

Trager, James. *The Women's Chronology.* New York: Henry Holt and Company, Inc., 1994.

Trudeau, Margaret. *Beyond Reason.* New York: Paddington Press, Ltd., 1979

Truman, Margaret. *First Ladies.* New York: Random House, Inc., 1995.

Wallace, Irving. *The Nympho and Other Maniacs.* New York: Simon and Schuster, 1971.

Warner, Carolyn. *The Last Word: A Treasury of Women's Quotes.* Englewood Cliffs, New Jersey: Prentice-Hall, Inc., 1992.

Weidenfeld, Sheila Rabb. *First Lady's Lady.* New York: G. P. Putnam's Sons, 1979.

West, J. B., and Mary Lynn Kotz. *Upstairs at the White House.* New York: Coward, McCann & Geoghegan, Inc., 1973.

Ziemann, Hugo. *The White House Cook Book.* Old Greenwich, Connecticut: The Devin Adair Company, 1983.

MAGAZINES

Gates, Henry Louis, Jr. "Hating Hillary." *The New Yorker,* February 26 and March 4, 1996.

Goodman, Susan. "Judith Martin." *Modern Maturity,* March–April 1996.

Goodwin, Doris Kearns. "The Home Front." *The New Yorker,* August 15, 1994.